COUNTERFACTUAL REASONING

A Basic Guide for Analysts, Strategists, and Decision Makers

The Proteus Monograph Series

Volume 2, Issue 5
October 2008

Proteus USA

The National Intelligence University, Office of the Director of National Intelligence and the Center for Strategic Leadership, U.S. Army War College established Proteus USA to focus on examining uncertainty, enhancing creativity, gaining foresight, and developing critical analytical and decision-making processes to effectively provide insight and knowledge to future complex national security, military, and intelligence challenges. The Group is also closely associated with Proteus and Foresight Canada.

The Proteus Monograph Series Fellows Program

The Proteus Monograph Series Fellows Program (PMSFP) funds research by scholars who are not affiliated with the U.S. Government and military. These scholars can be located either in the United States or abroad. This program is designed to support Proteus USA's charter to promote further discourse, study, and research focusing on the refinement, development, and application of new and emerging "futures" concepts, methods, processes, and scenarios. The overarching goal of this effort is to provide value-added and relevant commentary that will assist strategic and high-operational level decision makers, planners, and analysts with "outside the box" considerations and critical analysis of national, military and intelligence issues within the Joint, Interagency, Intergovernmental, and Multinational (JIIM) environment.

Counterfactual Reasoning: A Basic Guide for Analysts, Strategists, and Decision Makers

by

Noel Hendrickson, Ph.D.

Noel Hendrickson is Director of the Institute for National Security Analysis. This Institute is an academic research organization whose mission is to discover, develop, and deliver new analytic methods to the national security community. He also serves as Assistant Professor in the Information Analysis Program at James Madison University. The purpose of that program is to educate a new generation of intelligence analysts to engage multidimensional challenges with the most rigorous and innovative methods of analysis. As part of this program, he developed and now teaches a series of courses in advanced reasoning methods for defense and intelligence analysis, including "Hypothesis Testing," "Causal Analysis," "Counterfactual Reasoning," and "Strategy Assessment." He earned a Ph.D. in Philosophy from the University of Wisconsin in 2002. His early research focused on the structure and explanation of human action (especially how to understand the contingencies of decision making). His more recent work has been developing new approaches to critical thinking for analyzing information in the national security context. In addition to this book, he is a co-author of *Rowman and Littlefield's Handbook of Critical Thinking*, Rowman and Littlefield, 2008.

Acknowledgements

My initial work on counterfactual reasoning was done for (and in) my Fall 2005 "Counterfactuals" course. Thanks to Bill Hawk for allowing me the opportunity to test-run that course, and to all the students who participated.

This research was further developed (in a much more sophisticated fashion) over the Summer of 2006 and was supported by a grant from the Institute for Infrastructure and Information Assurance. Thanks to the Institute for their support on that project. In particular, I acknowledge the incredible significance of John Noftsinger and Ken Newbold, who put their trust in my research in its formative stages, when it would have been very easy not to notice it at all. I also appreciate the support of Jerry Benson, David T. Moore, Jay Hillmer, Mike Hutton, and Steve Stewart, who also offered encouragement on my work.

Some of the initial results from that work were presented at the "Descartes Conference on Mathematical Models in Counterterrorism" hosted by the Center for Advanced Defense Studies. Thanks to the Center for their support.

Above all, I must express my great appreciation to everyone associated with Proteus USA for their strong encouragement and the opportunity to further develop my work and to publish it. I am extremely grateful to Bill Wimbish, John Auger, Bill Waddell, and John Wheatley.

Finally, I acknowledge the importance of you, the reader, who has taken time out of your schedule to examine this work. It is my sincere hope that you will benefit from it. Indeed, one counterfactual that it is easy to affirm is: *if it had not been for the support of many other people, then this work would never have existed.*

Table of Contents

Executive Summary

Counterfactual reasoning is the process of evaluating conditional claims about alternate possibilities and their consequences (i.e., "What If" statements). These alternatives can be either past possibilities (e.g., "If the United States had not abolished the Iraqi army in 2003, then the Iraqi insurgency would have been significantly smaller in 2005") or future possibilities (e.g., "If Iran had nuclear weapons, then it would provide this technology to Hezbollah"). Counterfactuals are essential to intelligence analysis because they are implicit in all strategic assessments. For, any proposal about the appropriate response to a particular situation (past or future) assumes that certain things would or might occur if that response were made. However, at present, there is no comprehensive system of counterfactual reasoning to establish if these underlying assumptions are plausible. Such a system would have immense potential for analytic transformation as it could unite (or replace) a series of extant techniques of assessing alternate possibilities, such as "What If" Analysis, "High Impact/Low Probability" Analysis, and "Alternate Futures/Scenario" Analysis. And, ultimately, counterfactual reasoning represents the most ideal way to analyze possibilities, for it considers what would or might happen if the possibility were to occur, rather than attempting to determine if the possibility itself is probable.

The process of counterfactual reasoning has three stages. The first two of these are somewhat counterintuitive and are easily ignored by analysts. But, they are essential to structuring one's counterfactual reasoning properly. First, one must establish the particular way in which the alternate possibility comes to be (i.e., develop its "back-story"). Second, one must evaluate the events that occur between the time of the alternate possibility and the time for which one is considering its consequences. And third, one must examine the possible consequences of the alternate possibility's back-story and the events that follow it. In doing so, an analyst must connect their conclusion to the specific type of strategic assessment the counterfactual will be used to support: decision making under risk or decision making under uncertainty.

Counterfactual Reasoning

Chapter 1

Proposals for Counterfactual Reasoning

What if Iran had nuclear weapons? What if al-Qaida sympathizers staged a coup in Pakistan? What if the United States had not abolished the Iraqi army in 2003? What if the United States had taken al-Qaida's threats more seriously after the bombing of the USS Cole? Questions like these propose alternate possibilities: a sequence of events that could occur (or could have occurred) but have not (or did not). Because these events are possible, so are their consequences. This leads to a further series of questions such as: If Iran had nuclear weapons, would they pass on that technology to terrorists? Or, if the United States had not abolished the Iraqi army in 2003, would that have preempted the growth of the insurgency? And, because these possible consequences would be (or would have been) significant to U.S. interests, questions about them are critical to analysts, strategists, and decision makers.

A conditional claim about an alternate possibility and its consequences may be termed a "counterfactual." For example, the thesis that "If Iran had nuclear weapons, then it would provide this technology to Hezbollah" is a counterfactual claim. As well, the thesis that "If the United States had not abolished the Iraqi army in 2003, then the Iraqi insurgency would have been significantly smaller in 2005" is also a counterfactual claim. Both statements are proposals about alternate possibilities, their consequences, and the relationships between them. It is important to note that while the term "counterfactual" may seem to imply that the claim is "counter-to-fact," this need not be the case. Strictly speaking, a claim may be categorized as a counterfactual even if there is a chance it may come to pass, such as if it is about a future possibility. Thus, the term "counterfactual" can refer to any "subjunctive conditional" (i.e., any claim about what *would* or *might* occur in a particular possible alternative). Hence, any time an analyst proposes something of the form "If X were to occur, then Y would (or might) occur" and X is something that did not happen in the past and/

or has not (yet) happened in the future, then that analyst is engaging in *counterfactual reasoning*.[1]

Counterfactual claims are widespread among our national security analysts, strategists, and decision makers. Unfortunately, this is not widely recognized. Furthermore, there is no comprehensive model of counterfactual reasoning to which anyone may turn if they do become aware of the ubiquitous nature of counterfactuals within intelligence and national security. Instead, there are several fragmented approaches in philosophy, logic, history, political science, and psychology. To make matters worse, none of these approaches has been applied to the unique challenges of intelligence and security. In response, this work seeks to demonstrate both the *structure* and the *significance* of counterfactual reasoning. It offers not only the first complete system of counterfactual reasoning (of which this author is aware), but the first one specifically designed to address the domain of intelligence analysis and national security. Furthermore, this work proposes three major claims about the place of counterfactual reasoning in analysis and strategy. Therefore, this work is not only intended to serve as an *education in* counterfactual reasoning, but also as an *exhortation to* counterfactual reasoning.

It is important to keep the dual purpose of this work in mind. Some readers might not be persuaded of some of the more ambitious proposals made about the significance of counterfactual reasoning. In that case, it will remain perfectly possible for the reader still to employ the proposals about the structure of counterfactual reasoning unaltered. In other words, the system of how to do counterfactual reasoning appropriately is distinct from the three core proposals about the reasons why counterfactual reasoning matters to intelligence and national security. These proposals are made to motivate the reader both to use the system of counterfactual reasoning, and to think more broadly about the kinds of cognitive methods that should be used in general. Specifically, the central proposal of this work is this:

> **Central Proposal:** ***Counterfactual reasoning constitutes an essential component of analysis and strategy.***

This is a fairly bold proposal. If it is correct that counterfactual reasoning is *essential* to analysis and strategy, then that means *no* analysis or strategy can be done without reasoning counterfactually. In that case, educating analysts, strategists, and decision makers how to do counterfactual reasoning properly would be a vital task for anyone hoping to achieve "analytic transformation." Now, this central proposal is supported by three major claims about the role of counterfactual reasoning in intelligence analysis and national security.[2]

> **First Major Proposal (The Strategic Presumption of Counterfactuals):** ***All strategies (and analyses of them) are grounded in a series of counterfactual claims about alternate possibilities, their consequences, and the relationships between them.***

Counterfactual reasoning is essential to intelligence analysis and national security because all strategies (and analyses of them) are themselves grounded in counterfactual claims. Strategies *always presume* counterfactuals. As such, in order to formulate strategies reasonably, one has to employ the appropriate standards for counterfactual reasoning to ensure that the (counterfactual) grounding of those strategies is itself reasonable.

The *Strategic Presumption of Counterfactuals* is, in itself, sufficient to make counterfactual reasoning an essential component of analysis and strategy. Thus, any reader who is ultimately persuaded by the (forthcoming in chapter 2) arguments for this presumption, should also accept the central proposal. However, two additional claims will also be made that further demonstrate the significance of counterfactual reasoning.

> **Second Major Proposal (The Systematic Potential of Counterfactuals):** ***Major extant methods for assessing alternate possibilities, their consequences, and the relationships between them may be viewed as ultimately not distinct, but as aspects of a single process—counterfactual reasoning.***

Analysts already employ a number of well-known methods for assessing alternate possibilities. For example, they employ "What If" Analysis, "High Impact/Low Probability" Analysis, "Red Team" Analysis, "Gaming," and, of course, "scenario/Alternate Futures" Analysis.[3] At present, each of these techniques is utilized for slightly different kinds of problems. However, this work proposes that each of these techniques may be viewed as really just as different aspect of a single process, namely counterfactual reasoning. That is, the proposed model of counterfactual reasoning can unite (and/or replace) all of these distinct methods with one comprehensive process. Once again, I note that the model of counterfactual reasoning can serve as a useful one even if this turns out not to be the case. But, it should be clear that if the model is able to unite (and/or replace) all these disparate techniques, that would provide further evidence of the significance of counterfactual reasoning to intelligence analysis and national security.

Counterfactual reasoning provides a systematic approach to assessing alternate possibilities (especially those that underlie strategy). And, if the *Systematic Potential of Counterfactuals* turns out to be correct, then counterfactual reasoning may also subsume major extant methods for assessing alternate possibilities with a single one. But, neither of those claims means that counterfactual reasoning is the only method that one should employ for assessing alternate possibilities. That is the subject of the third (and most radical) proposal of this work.

> **Third Major Proposal (The Structural Priority of Counterfactuals):** ***All assessment of alternate possibilities, their consequences, and the relationships between them should ultimately be conditional (as it is in counterfactual reasoning).***

Not only can counterfactual reasoning unite (or replace) a number of well-known methods for assessing alternate possibilities, it is will further be proposed that counterfactual reasoning should replace all of these methods. More precisely, it will be argued (ultimately) that all assessment of alternate possibilities should be done in terms of conditionals (like counterfactuals) and never in any other terms. This is a fairly bold proposal, and it can be detached from the rest if needed. So, the reader can rest assured that, even if the arguments for it (in chapter 9) are not compelling, the credibility of the rest of this work remains unaffected.

To defend these three claims about the significance of counterfactual reasoning, as well as its structure, the work proceeds as follows. First, it explores the *purposes* of counterfactual reasoning (in order to disclose the relationship between counterfactuals and strategy). Second, it explains the *paradigms* of counterfactual reasoning (in order to demonstrate the need for a new approach). Third, it explicates the *problems* of counterfactual reasoning (in order to describe the three major stages of reasoning counterfactually). Fourth, it elucidates the *prospects* of counterfactual reasoning (to display how these three major stages capture what is being done in each of the major extant approaches to analyzing alternate possibilities). Fifth, it establishes the *procedures* of counterfactual reasoning (of each of the three stages). Sixth, it examines the *practices* of counterfactual reasoning and how they can make a difference to intelligence (in greater detail for one of the major domains to which it is applied: proactive strategy assessment). And seventh, it explicates some *pitfalls* of counterfactual reasoning (that arise in its more advanced versions).

Before continuing, it is important to make a few qualifications. First, as already noted, this work offers both a systematic approach to counterfactual reasoning and a series of proposals about the role of counterfactual reasoning in intelligence analysis and national security. These two aspects of the work are separable. It is possible for one to be true even if the other turns out to be inadequate (in part or in whole). Thus, *even if this work errs in terms of its assessment of the significance of counterfactual reasoning, that says nothing about its assessment of the structure of counterfactual reasoning (and vice versa).* Second, this work is intended to be a *basic* guide. That is, it is intended to be the sort of thing someone could read on their own, or employ in a "professional development" short-course. It is not exhaustive. Thus, for example, in the author's semester-long "Counterfactual Reasoning" course, there are many more subjects taken up that have been left out of this work (for the sake of space). So, this work should not be taken as the complete story on counterfactual reasoning, but only as addressing the foundations. Third, this is intended primarily for those who are already working in intelligence analysis or national security (or hoping to be so). As such, there are many theoretical questions that are set aside, since they are not directly relevant to this audience. While there are many bold philosophical claims implicit in this work, discussion of them (*qua* philosophy) has been set aside for another occasion, again, for the sake of space.

Chapter 2

Purposes of Counterfactual Reasoning

Finding the answers to "what if" questions is an intriguing endeavor. As such, some regard counterfactual reasoning to be worth doing strictly for its own sake. However, intelligence and national security analysts rarely have the liberty to pursue intellectual activities purely for their inherent worth. Instead, their analysis is always for some grander purpose, which ultimately is to inform their customer on a vital subject to enhance decision making. Thus, counterfactual reasoning's value for analysis and strategy will have to be for the benefits that it confers on that process. And, counterfactual theorists, while not directly addressing intelligence or national security, have proposed a number of purposes for counterfactual reasoning that are relevant to analysis and strategy.

The first and most commonly cited purpose for counterfactual reasoning is to facilitate causal analysis. Many philosophers and social scientists are interested in counterfactuals because they think there is a connection between causal dependence and counterfactual dependence.[4] For example, suppose that it were the case that "If the United States had not abolished the Iraqi army in 2003, then the Iraqi insurgency would have been much smaller in 2005." That means that the size of the Iraqi insurgency in 2005 is counterfactually dependent on the abolishing of the Iraqi army in 2003. (In general, Y is counterfactually dependent on X means that: If X had not occurred, then Y would not have occurred.) Some would be prepared to infer from this that the abolishing of the Iraqi army in 2003 is one of the causes of the size of the Iraqi insurgency in 2005. In other words, counterfactual dependence implies causal dependence.

Causal claims are widespread in intelligence and national security. Frequently, strategists and decision makers have only the resources to intervene in one or two ways in order to try to bring about the effects that they desire. Thus, they need to know what the most significant causal forces are that are relevant to those desired effects. Therefore, causal analysis is a vital task for analysis and strategy. So, if counterfactual dependence does imply causal dependence, then counterfactual reasoning would also be incredibly useful for analysis and strategy. It would offer an important tool for a vital reasoning challenge: causal analysis.[5]

The second purpose for counterfactual reasoning is to overcome deterministic biases. Psychologists and other social scientists have demonstrated a human tendency to regard past events as far more inevitable than they actually were.[6] It is easy to think that what occurred could not have possibly been avoided. The indeterminacies of the past are easily hidden once the outcome is known. But, the fact that one thing actually did happen does not mean that only one thing was possible or even plausible. The propensity to regard what actually happened as inevitable when it was not, or even more probable than it was, is often termed "hindsight bias." Anyone concerned with an accurate view of history would regard such bias as a worrisome tendency, and anyone concerned with a plausible view of the future would regard it as downright dangerous. For, if the past is always regarded as inevitable (or much more probable than it really was), then the future is likely to be taken to be so also. Just as one can regard what did happen as inevitable when it was not, one can also regard what one predicts will happen as inevitable when it is not. There is also a human tendency for a "foresight bias."

Analysts and strategists cannot avoid having a view of history and a view of what will occur in the future. But, if those paradigms are contaminated with a sense that those events are inevitable (when they surely are not), the resulting assessments and decisions are equally suspect. Counterfactual reasoning can serve as a useful antidote to these tendencies. For, if one works through the various ways that a particular event would not (or will not) occur, then one will thereby have to recognize that the event is not inevitable. There are ways that the event might not (or even would not) happen. Hence, counterfactual reasoning offers a further useful function for analysis and strategy: increased recognition of indeterminacies.

A third purpose for counterfactual reasoning is to incorporate creativity into the analytic process. In response to recent intelligence failures, it has become somewhat common to charge analysts with a lack of creativity of thought, imagination, or openness to other possibilities.[7] Unfortunately, this is a rather shallow criticism, as surely analysts are trying to consider various options and obviously have the mental faculties necessary to imagine all sorts of possibilities. If there is a problem here, it is presumably not a "failure of imagination." Instead, it would seem to be a failure of the underlying reasoning techniques that analysts use to incorporate their imaginative options into the analytic process. For, it is one thing to come up with interesting possibilities; it is another to have a way to systematically integrate them into one's analysis. If there is a problem of creativity in analysis and strategy, it would be not with the analysts, but with the methods they employ.

Strategies in intelligence and national security have substantial consequences, and thus it is only reasonable that analysts are cautious about including the lively possibilities that they might imagine. For creativity to be relevant to intelligence there has to be a way to incorporate it reliably into the analytic process, which requires that there be a rigorous way to do so. The system of counterfactual reasoning that is proposed here is intended to do just that. It offers a structured way to rigorously assess alternate possibilities and their consequences. It requires analysts to think creatively, but also to connect their creative thinking to a series of precise techniques so that it *never becomes speculation*. Thus, counterfactual reasoning offers a third important benefit to analysis and strategy: a way to rigorously employ creative thinking.

Facilitating causal analysis, mitigating deterministic biases, and incorporating creativity are all valuable purposes for counterfactual reasoning. However, none of them are the most critical function of counterfactual reasoning in analysis and strategy. In fact, this work regards all three of these purposes to be of secondary importance. Instead, the most vital purpose of counterfactual reasoning is to ground strategic assessment. This relates directly to the first major proposal about counterfactual reasoning: the *Strategic Presumption of Counterfactuals* (i.e., All strategies, and analyses of them, are grounded in a series of counterfactual claims about alternate possibilities, their consequences, and the relationships between them). Counterfactual reasoning is essential to analysis and strategy most fundamentally because *all strategic assessment and/or decision making presupposes counterfactual claims.*

Suppose that the Iranian regime continues to be hostile to American interests and to pursue nuclear power and the underlying technology that would make it feasible to develop nuclear weapons in a short period of time. And suppose that intelligence and security strategists propose that the United States go beyond mere economic sanctions in response. That recommendation only makes sense if it is assumed that, for example, "If the United States responds only with economic sanctions, then Iran will not deviate from its current path." For, if one had assumed (instead) that if the United States continued merely with economic sanctions, then Iran would back off, then there would be no reason to recommend something more serious. That is to say, the strategic recommendation assumes a counterfactual claim about what would occur in a particular possible situation.

Now, this is not the only counterfactual claim that is assumed in this situation. One also assumes something like "If Iran continues to develop nuclear power as it is presently doing, then Iran would eventually develop nuclear weapons technology." If one assumed that Iran was only interested in nuclear power and had no desire for nuclear weapons technology whatsoever, then there would be far less reason to be concerned about their nuclear program. The significance that is attached to the question of what to do about their program only makes sense if one assumes what they would end up with if they continued. And, that, of course, assumes a further counterfactual claim about what Iran would or might do if they had nuclear weapons technology (e.g., that they would pass the technology on to terrorists, or use their weapons against U.S. interests, or create a nuclear arms race in the Middle East, etc.). For, if one assumes that Iran would not do anything negative whatsoever with nuclear weapons technology, then there would be far less reason to be concerned about paths that might lead to it.

To put the matter more generally, every strategic question that one might ask has a series of counterfactual assumptions underneath it. To be concerned about the question "What should we do about X?" assumes something along the lines of "If X is allowed to occur and/or to continue, then Y would or might occur" (where Y is something that impinges upon one's interests). In a similar fashion, any assessment of the question "What should we do about X?" also makes a series of counterfactual assumptions. Just as the proposal that more than economic sanctions are necessary to deter Iran assumes that merely using economic sanctions will not work, any assessment of possible decisions will include assumptions about *what would (or might) happen if that decision were to be made.* Therefore, any assessment of whether to do A, B, or C in response to X will assume things of the form "If we were to do A in response to X, then Z would or might occur," and "If we were to do B in response to X, then Z* would or might occur." and so on. To push things even further, for every D, E, and F that one is not considering as a response to X, there will also be a series of claims about what would occur if one did one of those (at a minimum, that it would not achieve the relevant goals).

Therefore, all strategic assessment and decision making will have at least two layers of underlying counterfactual claims. First, there will be implicit counterfactual claims establishing the significance of the topic being considered (i.e., what would or might occur if that thing continues or changes). Second, there will be implicit counterfactual claims about the consequences of each of the possible decisions that are being considered (i.e., what would or might occur if that decision were made). In addition, in many cases, there will be two further layers of underlying counterfactual claims. First, there may be implicit counterfactual claims about why the consequences of the present topic are significant (i.e., what would happen if the imagined consequences were to obtain). Second, there may be implicit counterfactual claims about the consequences of other possible decisions that are not being considered (i.e., at a minimum, that if those decisions were made, they would not positively affect the outcome of interest).

It is important to note that strategic assessment need not always be directly connected to decision making. Sometimes analysts evaluate possible decisions not to guide an immediate decision, but to provide more general insights on decision making for unspecified future decisions. This is frequently the case with evaluations of past decisions. Security analysts (especially with a military/defense focus) frequently engage in "after action" reports where they reconstruct a past situation to determine whether the best decisions were in fact made. They want to know if things could have been done differently in order to avoid any negative outcomes that occurred, and/or if things could have been done differently and still maintained any positive outcomes that occurred. This may often be done to guide very similar immediately future cases, but it can also be done to form more general strategies about how to handle specific kinds of cases, even if it is not known when they would arise. This clearly is just as much as dependent upon underlying counterfactual claims as is strategic assessment with future possibilities. For, one still must determine what would or might occur if each possible decision is made, as well as why the subject being considered is itself significant (what the implications are of its continuing or changing).

One of the most vital goals of intelligence and national security analysis is to foster well-justified strategic assessment and decision making. But, every attempt at strategic assessment and/or decision making is grounded in a series of counterfactual claims. So, if that strategic

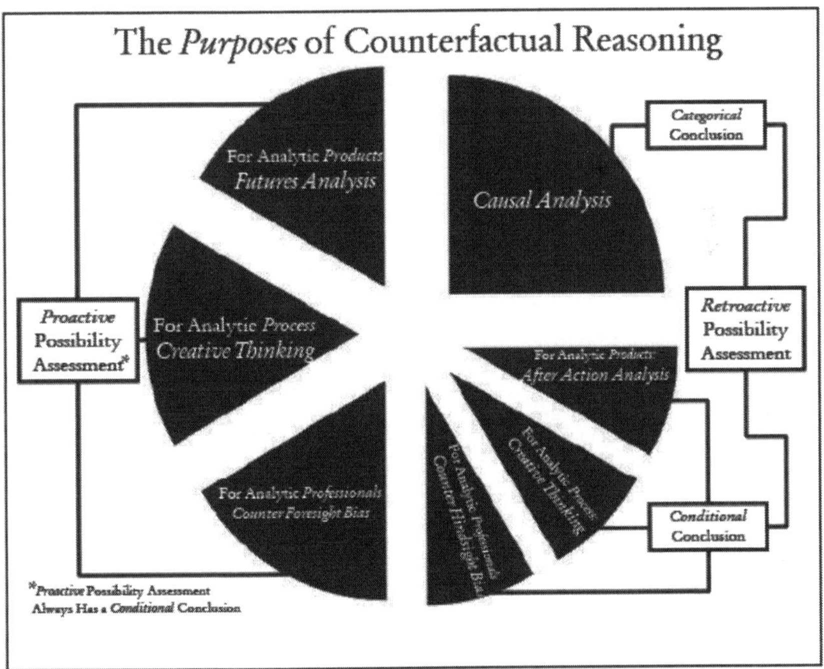

Figure 1: Chart of the major purposes of counterfactual reasoning as discussed in this chapter. Note that the size of the pieces of the chart do not represent the relative importance of that purpose. Also note, however, that half of the chart is devoted to proactive and the other half is devoted to retroactive possibility assessment.

assessment and/or decision making is to be well justified, then those underlying counterfactual claims must also be well justified. Hence, if intelligence and national security analysis is to foster well-justified strategic assessment and decision making, then it most also exemplify well-justified counterfactual reasoning. For this reason, this work concludes that *counterfactual reasoning constitutes an essential component of analysis and strategy* (i.e., the central proposal about counterfactual reasoning is true).

Chapter 3

Paradigms of Counterfactual Reasoning

There are three major extant paradigms of counterfactual reasoning. While each of these has something important to contribute to understanding counterfactuals, none are able to provide a systematic guide to well-justified counterfactual reasoning for analysis and strategy. As a result, this work develops the first (of which this author is aware) comprehensive attempt at a fourth paradigm.

The first (and oldest) paradigm of counterfactual reasoning is the conceptual approach. This paradigm derives from philosophy and logic. Its primary purpose is to offer a theory of the concept of a counterfactual.[8] That purpose is often part of a larger philosophical project of offering an account of all the core concepts humans have of the world around them. Or, the purpose could be more narrow in terms of simply offering an account of the concept of causation (when the philosopher thinks counterfactual dependence implies causation). Or, the purpose could be even more narrow, simply to offer a proposal about what makes certain subjunctive (i.e., counterfactual) conditionals true and others false. But, regardless of the ultimate purpose, the major effort in this paradigm is to understand the conditions that make counterfactual statements true or false (as well to understand the logical relationships between them).

One might think that seeking to know the conditions that make counterfactual claims true or false would be directly relevant to counterfactual reasoning in analysis and strategy. However, this is not entirely true. For, when philosophers seek to know the "truth conditions" of counterfactual statements, they are not seeking to know how one goes about determining if a particular counterfactual is true or false. Instead, they are trying to understand a more general matter: how counterfactuals can *be* true or false. So, instead of offering a procedure for determining the truth or falsity of a specific counterfactual, philosophers and logicians seek to explore what it is about reality that would make it possible for there to be counterfactuals that are true or false in the first place. Thus, one would consider (for example) things like the concept of a "possible world" (i.e., way that reality might have been). The "possible worlds" theory is a well-known account of counterfactuals (in the conceptual approach) in which a counterfactual is true based on what is true in the closest possible world(s) to ours.[9] That is to say, counterfactuals are true based on similarity relations that hold between possible ways that the world might have been. Now, it is possible to derive certain kinds of general rules from that for how to explore specific counterfactuals. But, it is not a goal of this paradigm to expose such rules. This paradigm is metaphysical (attempting to describe reality) and not epistemological (attempting to describe how we know reality). Therefore, while this approach should be taken seriously in terms of the logical or conceptual questions it poses about counterfactuals, it is not directly concerned with what is necessary for analysis and strategy: a way to determine whether specific counterfactual claims are reasonably believed to be true or false.

The second paradigm of counterfactual reasoning is the descriptive approach. This paradigm derives from social and cognitive psychology. Its primary purpose is to offer a theory of how the typical human thinks about counterfactuals.[10] That purpose is often part of a larger project for how humans actually (and typically) reason. Or, that purpose could be motivated by further theories that counterfactual thinking plays an important role for humans, such as to aid coping with difficult situations (e.g., by recognizing that a negative outcome could have been worse, or could not have turned out any better). Part of this could involve exposing the biases that often emerge when humans think about alternate possibilities (such as hindsight bias). But, regardless of the purpose, this paradigm is focused on describing the actual way that humans (typically) think about alternate possibilities, their consequences, and the relationships between them.

Much like the conceptual approach, the descriptive approach might initially seem directly relevant to the project of guiding counterfactual reasoning for analysis and strategy. However, it too is not exactly what the analyst needs. While it is useful to understand how humans often reason about counterfactuals, the ultimate goal of the analyst is to form well-justified counterfactual claims to develop well-justified strategies and sound decisions. And, there is no reason to assume that the way humans typically reason counterfactually is also well justified (in fact, quite the opposite). The famous "naturalistic fallacy" looms large here.

That is, the fact that something *is* the case does not provide evidence that that something *should be* the case. There is an "is/ought" gap: how we do reason may not be how we should reason. It is useful to know that humans have a tendency to regard things as more inevitable than they were or are, but that does not suffice to provide a systematic approach to how to assess alternate possibilities. Thus, the descriptive approach also is not directly concerned with what is necessary for analysis and strategy: a way to determine whether specific counterfactual claims are reasonably believed to be true or false.

The third paradigm of counterfactual reasoning is the practical approach. This paradigm derives from political science and history. Its primary purpose is to determine the plausibility of particular historically important counterfactual claims.[11] This may sometimes have a narrow purpose of simply exploring something of particular interest to a specific social scientist, but it is often part of a larger view in which counterfactuals are important to establishing causal claims or to recognizing the indeterminacies of history. Now, in order to determine whether a counterfactual is a plausible one for social scientific purposes, this paradigm attempts to offer basic rules for assessing counterfactual claims. However, it is important to note that the fundamental purpose of this paradigm is not to offer a systematic theory of how to reason counterfactually, but to assess the plausibility of specific counterfactuals in the context of the social sciences.

Of all three extant paradigms, the practical approach may seem most directly relevant to analysis and strategy. And, perhaps this is the case. However, it is still ultimately inadequate. For, there is a significant difference between being plausible enough to admit into social scientific discussion and being plausible enough to ground a well-justified strategic assessment. The latter is a much more difficult goal to achieve, and hence requires a much more stringent standard. And, it is not the goal of the practical approach to offer such rules. In the practical approach, any guiding principles that are offered are simply a means to an end; they are not the goal of the inquiry. There is no aspiration towards a systematic account of the principles of well-justified counterfactual reasoning. So, the practical approach also is not directly concerned with what is necessary for analysis and strategy: a way to determine whether specific counterfactual claims are reasonably believed to be true or false.

Strategic assessments in intelligence and national security have to be as well justified as is possible. But, well-justified conclusions are rarely an accident. Instead, they derive from the application of a system of reliable reasoning principles. Unfortunately, none of the three extant paradigms of counterfactual reasoning seek to provide that for counterfactuals. Thus, it is no surprise that there is not (yet) a complete system for how to reason counterfactually. Therefore, counterfactual reasoning for analysis and strategy suggests the need for a fourth paradigm: the prescriptive approach. This paradigm is transdisciplinary. It draws from all relevant insights from philosophy, logic, psychology, history, political science, and the new emerging discipline of intelligence studies/information analysis. Its goal is a set of criteria that will enable analysts to determine whether specific counterfactual claims can be reasonably believed to be true or false. And, this is done so that those analysts can formulate well-justified strategic assessments to guide decision makers.

Unlike the practical approach, the prescriptive approach is not (in itself) concerned with the truth or falsity of any specific counterfactuals. Instead, it is concerned with the criteria by which one may determine the truth or falsity of specific counterfactuals. Unlike the descriptive approach, the prescriptive approach is not (in itself) focused on how humans actually reason counterfactually. Instead it is focused on how humans *should* reason counterfactually. And, unlike the conceptual approach, the prescriptive approach is not (in itself) concerned with the concept of a counterfactual or what it is about reality that makes counterfactual statements true or false. Instead, it is concerned with how an analyst can come to know (or reasonably believe) that a counterfactual statement is true of false. Thus, while all three extant approaches are connected to the process of counterfactual reasoning, none directly addresses the most fundamental need of the intelligence and national security analyst. Only the prescriptive approach has as its distinct focus the discovery of *a way to determine whether specific counterfactual claims can be reasonably believed to be true or false.*

Chapter 4

Problems of Counterfactual Reasoning

One of the most important elements of developing a systematic approach to counterfactual reasoning is to define the fundamental challenges to sound thinking about counterfactuals. Thus, this work begins constructing a fourth paradigm for counterfactual reasoning by defining the two essential problems of counterfactual reasoning.

There are three components to every counterfactual claim. The first part of the counterfactual is called the *antecedent*. The second part is called the *consequent*. And the relationship that is affirmed between the two is the *modal connection*. So, in the counterfactual "If Iran were to develop nuclear weapons technology, then it would provide this technology to Hezbollah," the antecedent is "Iran develops nuclear weapons technology." The antecedent identifies the specific possibility whose consequences are under evaluation. The consequent of that counterfactual is "Iran provides nuclear weapons technology to Hezbollah." The consequent identifies the consequence that the counterfactual purports to be connected to the possibility of the antecedent. The modal connection of the counterfactual is "would." That is, the obtaining of the antecedent would be followed by the obtaining of the consequent. (The other possible modal connection, which is not used in this counterfactual but is relevant to others, is "might.")

There is a great temptation for new counterfactual reasoners to hold that the fundamental challenge is to determine which (if any) modal connection holds between a specific antecedent and consequent. However, while this is a challenge, it is *not* a major challenge. A slightly more experience counterfactual reasoner is likely to suggest that a major challenge would be to determine what sorts of possibilities are worth considering as consequents in the counterfactual. And, while this is a slightly more important challenge, this also is *not* a major challenge. Someone who is aware of these two things not being major challenges might propose that the major challenge is determining what antecedents are worthy of being considering in counterfactual claims. And, that is an important challenge. For often analysts fail to consider the right sorts of possibilities, often because they fail to generate the right options in the first place. However, that is not so much a challenge for counterfactual reasoning as it for possibility generation in general. So, surprisingly enough, finding antecedents, consequents, and appropriate modal connections are not major challenges in counterfactual reasoning.

The very things that seem initially to be plausible candidates for the major challenges to counterfactual reasoning turn out (as shall be seen) not to be especially difficult problems at all. And instead, the most substantial problems are ultimately two things that very often do not even occur to anyone unless they are pointed out. Just as counterfactual claims themselves can easily go unnoticed as they lie implicitly underneath strategic assessments, so too the major challenges of counterfactual reasoning can also go unnoticed as they lie implicitly underneath "common-sense" counterfactual thinking. As such, to formulate well-justified counterfactual claims, one has to structure one's reasoning in a seemingly counterintuitive way. One has to focus on two problems that are not likely to occur to the unaided mind. Counterfactual reasoning is an excellent example of a kind of thinking where, if one does not ask the right questions, one has almost no chance of getting the right answers, regardless of how hard or long one attempts to think about it. This point cannot be emphasized enough. As such, it will be made into the first of this work's twenty proposed counterfactual reasoning principles.

> **Counterfactual Reasoning Principle 1:** ***The degree to which one's ultimate counterfactual claim is justified is largely due to the extent to which one has structured the counterfactual reasoning process to address the most significant challenges to effective counterfactual reasoning.***

Before one can reasonably begin to consider what sorts of consequents are worth considering, let alone what sort of modal connection might hold between that consequent and the antecedent, one has to first have a more precise understanding of to what the antecedent refers. For example, the antecedent "Iran develops nuclear weapons technology" seems like a perfectly reasonable statement. An analyst, especially one who is a specialist on Iran or nuclear weapons technology, is likely to think that they understand perfectly well what that statement means. However, there is a hidden ambiguity in the statement that must be resolved before any further thinking on what sorts of consequents might be connected to this antecedent. For, there are a number of different ways that it could be true that "Iran develops nuclear weapons technology." And to say "If Iran were to develop nuclear weapons technology, then it would provide this technology to Hezbollah" does not specify which of those ways is being postulated as the possibility.

For example, Iran could develop nuclear weapons technology totally on their own without any outside assistance. Or, Iran could develop nuclear weapons technology with the assistance of a foreign government that also has nuclear weapons technology. Or, Iran could develop nuclear weapons technology with the assistance of materials it purchased from the black market. Or, Iran could develop nuclear weapons technology with the assistance of materials or knowledge it steals from another nuclear power. And, of course, this is only the beginning of the possibilities. One can also consider the relationship between this and Iranian nuclear power initiatives. Iran could develop nuclear weapons technology as an afterthought of, or as an appendix to, its nuclear power program. Or, Iran could develop nuclear weapons technology as the primary purpose of a purely superficial nuclear power initiative. And, of course, there are other options in between. In addition, Iran could develop nuclear weapons technology in defiance of serious UN sanctions, or without serious UN sanctions (and many other options in between).

Thus, the mere selection of an antecedent for counterfactual consideration is only a very rough description of the sort of possibility one will be considering. To do any sort of rigorous reasoning about that possibility, one has to have a full account of *how that possibility came to be*. From all the different ways that the antecedent might be true, one has to select one (or a small number of them) to be the subject of the counterfactual reasoning. One cannot have any sort of rigorous counterfactual reasoning with only the mere statement of the possibility that comes from the antecedent alone. One has to have an entire *antecedent scenario*. In the case of a future possibility, this scenario would be a complete story that begins from the present (or even further back) and leads up to the moment at which the antecedent becomes true. In the case of a past alternate possibility, this scenario would begin with a deviation from actual history and then chart an alternate course of history up until the time at which the antecedent becomes true. The antecedent scenario is the "back-story" of the counterfactual. These antecedent scenarios can be simple or complex, short or long; it all depends on the specific antecedent in question.

One could propose that there really is no need for such detail in constructing a counterfactual argument for a specific strategic assessment. However, it is important to consider the factors that must be present to make that argument a rigorous and plausible one. To make any sort of well-justified conclusion about the consequences of, for example, a nuclear-armed Iran, one has to (at a minimum) have some sense of their intentions for such technology. But, that will vary widely depending upon how they came to achieve such technology. A nuclear Iran that happened on it by accident is likely to be different from one that stole the technology from a rival. A nuclear Iran that defied major UN sanctions is likely to be different from one that did not. All those details have at least the potential to make a significant difference to the consequents and modal connections that are selected. And, one cannot simply arbitrarily pick one of the possibilities, for perhaps one of the others will be more critical or useful. One's selection of antecedent scenarios makes a significant difference (at least potentially, if not probably) to the ultimate counterfactual claim one makes. As such, analysts must have a serious set of procedures to apply to *select antecedent scenarios*. This is the first major challenge in counterfactual reasoning.

Once one has specified a particular antecedent scenario (or small set thereof), one will again be tempted to move on to determining what consequents and/or modal connections are appropriately justified by that antecedent. But, once again, this would be a major mistake. There is a second hidden ambiguity that must be resolved if rigorous counterfactual reasoning is to be possible. For example, one would typically not merely be interested in the consequences of a nuclear-armed Iran *the day they achieve nuclear weapons technology*. Instead, one would likely be interested in the consequences over the next few months, years, or even decades. Thus, there is often a significant difference between the time at which the antecedent becomes true (the antecedent scenario ends) and the timing of consequents that are being considered (when the *consequent scenario* begins). So, there will be a large number of events during that intermediate period between the time of the antecedent and the time of the possible consequent.

The events that make up that intermediate period, or *intermediate states,* are critical to the ultimate plausibility of the counterfactual. As a result, one has to be extremely careful about what intermediate states are affirmed. And, there are only three options as to how one might find such intermediate states. First, these events could be those that actually happened after the time at which the antecedent would be true (in the case of a past alternate possibility). Second, these events could be independently projected to happen after the time at which the antecedent would become true (in the case of a future alternate possibility). Or, third, these events could be the consequents of other true counterfactuals that have the same antecedents as the one under consideration. (i.e., part of what would happen during the 10 years after Iran obtained nuclear weapons technology would include what would happen after 5 years of its having nuclear weapons technology). The last of these three options is "supporting counterfactuals," which are established to be true by means of the entire process of counterfactual reasoning. The former two options are a matter for a specific aspect of the counterfactual reasoning process. They pose the second major challenge to counterfactual reasoning.

In the case of a future possibility, such as the 10 year consequences of a nuclear-armed Iran, there will be many other events that are independently projected (or held to be plausible) to occur during that time. For example, there will be assessments about the United States and Canada, the United States and North Korea, the United States and Iraq, and so forth. But, those projections will be (in all likelihood) made *without assuming that Iran would have nuclear weapons technology.* As such, one cannot assume these projections would still be plausible if Iran did come to have such weapons. For example, a projection about the U.S. relationship with Iraq would presumably be very different depending on whether it had a nuclear neighbor. In a similar fashion, one cannot assume that none of the projections would still be plausible if Iran had nuclear weapons. Presumably, an economic projection about the U.S. relationship with Canada could plausibly still be the same if Iran had nuclear weapons (although it might not, of course). Then, there are cases that could easily go in either direction, such as the U.S. relationship with other nuclear (or possibly nuclear) powers of which it is suspicious, such as North Korea. The same holds with past possibilities. If the United States had not abolished the Iraqi army in 2003, there are some things that happened in the intervening years that would plausibly not have still happened if it kept the Iraqi army intact, and there are others that plausibly would have still happened if the Iraqi army had remained intact.

Since much of the plausibility of a counterfactual argument will derive from the number of events that one can employ as support for (or against) a particular outcome, the choice of events during (for example) a 10 year period between an antecedent scenario and a consequent scenario is absolutely vital to forming well-justified counterfactual claims. An analyst must have a way to sort out those events that did (or were projected to) occur during that period that should remain even if the antecedent scenario holds *from those that should not remain if the antecedent scenario holds.* Analysts need a set of procedures to apply to *select intermediate states*. This is the second major challenge to counterfactual reasoning.

Because these two challenges are so critical to counterfactual reasoning, and so easy (and intuitive) for analysts to skip over, this work structures the procedures of counterfactual reasoning into three stages: those that address the first challenge, those that address the second challenge, and those that address everything else. This may seem like a radical move, but counterfactual reasoning is so vital to well-justified strategic assessments, and these two problems are so vital to counterfactual reasoning, that they have to remain always in the forefront of the analyst's reasoning if there is any chance of achieving well-justified strategic assessments.

Therefore, the proposed system of counterfactual reasoning affirms three stages. First, there is *antecedent scenario selection.* In this stage, one determines the "back-story" for the antecedent by means of assessing (from all the possible options) how it comes to be. Second, there is *intermediate state selection.* In this stage, one determines which events that did occur (or are independently projected to occur) during the time between the antecedent and consequent also occur even when the antecedent is true. And third, there is *consequent scenario selection.*

In this stage, one determines which consequents stand in the modal connections of "would" or "might" with the antecedent (i.e., what would or might occur). In this stage, and in this stage alone, one searches for what would happen if that antecedent came to be.

One final note should be made. Obviously, there are other problems for counterfactual reasoning besides these two major ones. For example, when this work comes to the third stage, there will turn out to be a number of important issues that analysts must be diligent to address. And, of course, there are important questions to be asked about how to come up with antecedents that are worthy of being considered in the first place. However, one of the most important claims about counterfactual reasoning that this work hopes to make is that *the degree to which one's ultimate counterfactual claim is justified is largely due to the extent to which one structured the counterfactual reasoning process to address the most significant challenges to effective counterfactual reasoning.* And that demands that one focus a large portion (if not most) of one's counterfactual reasoning effort on antecedent scenario selection and intermediate state selection. Those are the two major problems of counterfactual reasoning.

The *Problems* of Counterfactual Reasoning

Three Stages of Counterfactual Reasoning

Antecedent X — Consequent Y

Break with Prior History

Antecedent Scenario for X

Intermediate States

Consequent Scenario for Y

Continuation to Future

Counterfactual: *'If X were to occur, then Y would (or might) occur.'*

1. Select Antecedent Scenario	2. Select Intermediate States	3. Select Consequent Scenario
Explore the ways the antecedent could have come to be, determine which constitutes the relevant antecedent scenario (back-story)	Examine intermediate events that hold between antecedent and consequent, establish those that also hold in the alternate history	Evaluate the possible outcomes to establish those that would/might occur given the antecedent and intermediate states

Figure 2: Chart describing the major problems of counterfactual reasoning. These two major problems set up the three stages of counterfactual reasoning (by forming the first two).

Chapter 5

Prospects for Counterfactual Reasoning

Antecedent scenario selection and intermediate state selection determine the three major stages of counterfactual reasoning, and they also foster much of the ambitious prospects of counterfactual reasoning. For, as this section will propose (and later sections demonstrate), it is possible for counterfactual reasoning to unite a series of disparate widely used techniques for evaluating possibilities into a comprehensive system. In other words, once one recognizes the three major stages of counterfactual reasoning, one can thereby determine that a number of structured analytic techniques for assessing possibilities are actually not distinct processes, but different parts of a single process: counterfactual reasoning. (Note: This work will assume that the reader has some at least rough familiarity with each of these techniques. As such, they will only be described in sufficient detail to illustrate that they can be understood to actually be different pieces of the overall counterfactual reasoning process.)[12]

Two of the most popular structured analytic techniques for evaluating possibilities are "High Impact/Low Probability" Analysis and (most famously) "Alternate Futures/Scenario" Analysis. These techniques are typically regarded to be distinct cognitive strategies. However, they are actually just slightly different cases of one stage of counterfactual reasoning. In "High Impact/Low Probability" Analysis, an analyst has identified a very specific possibility that is not especially probable, but would seem to have (potentially at least) very dramatic consequences for their customer's interests. Then, the analyst attempts to determine the consequences of that specific possibility. Ultimately, if done properly, this technique is simply striving to achieve the third stage of counterfactual reasoning: consequent scenario selection. The analyst already has a very detailed account of the possibility (antecedent scenario) and its immediate aftermath (intermediate states), all that remains is the long-term consequences (i.e., consequent scenarios).

"Alternate Futures/Scenario" Analysis offers a way for analysts to map out what might occur in the future. Here the object is also consequent scenario selection. However, there is a more narrow focus on consequents that might obtain (rather than those that would obtain. In addition, there is no particular possibility that is singled out from the start as initiating the scenarios (as there is on "High Impact/Low Probability" Analysis). In other words, there already is an antecedent scenario and set of intermediate states made up of "if things proceed as they currently are" (alternatively, one could, of course, specify a particular set of alternatives in the "drivers" that one selects to determine the four or eight scenarios that one will formulate). Thus, both "High Impact/Low Probability" and "Alternate Futures/Scenario" Analysis can be reinterpreted as simply an attempt to focus in on one element of counterfactual reasoning: consequent scenario selection.

Other popular structured techniques for evaluating possibilities, such as "What If" Analysis, also map onto counterfactual reasoning. This structured analytic technique is designed to identify a plausible path to a particularly interesting (even if improbable) possibility. For example, one might wonder about how a secular democracy might arise in Iran. In such a case, one is not asking about the consequences of such a possibility (interesting though those might be), but instead how that possibility might come to be. This is an example of how an analyst might (without realizing it) be asking about antecedent scenario selection. One has a general possibility but needs to develop a "back-story" for how it came to be. That is much like the first stage of counterfactual reasoning.

Another pair of popular structured techniques for evaluating possibilities is "Red Team" Analysis and "Gaming." In both of these approaches, one also has a very precise set of possibilities that one wishes to consider the consequences of (like on "High Impact/Low Probability" Analysis), but this time the analysts are selected on the basis of also having some specialized subject-matter expertise in the kind of case being considered, and also (in "Gaming") there is an attempt to actually simulate how the actual actors would (or might) act out in reality. Thus, both of these techniques also would fall into the third stage of counterfactual reasoning (consequent scenario selection), with the addition that the participants have specialized subject expertise in the area under consideration and (in "Gaming") that there is an attempt to simulate (via acting things out) what the participants would do.

A further structure analytic technique that this author has (elsewhere) advocated is "structured Scenario Fusion."[13] The purpose of that process is to unite distinct futures estimates made by different analysts on different subjects into a single projection. One of the major challenges of this process is the need to unite assessments that have different underlying assumptions. One has to assess how the events in the assessment would be affected *if different precipitating assumptions had been made.* This is very much like the process of intermediate state selection. One has to assess the impact of a different antecedent on things that were independently projected to occur (e.g., whether they are still plausible to affirm, or if different assessments now become plausible).

Counterfactual reasoning has the potential to offer a comprehensive system for evaluating alternate possibilities, their consequences, and the relationships between them. It has the prospect of uniting six different structured analytic techniques into a single process. This is an extremely important benefit of employing counterfactual reasoning. Now an analyst who is interested in a specific task, such as how one might come to have a secular regime in Iran or how a specific future battle that is precisely described might play out, can employ a reasoning strategy that is not "stove-piped" narrowly for that task. Instead, they can place their narrow reasoning project in the context of a comprehensive system. In so doing, they would see that there might be a need to connect their individual project up with other projects by other analysts. Or, they might see that they have conceived their project incorrectly in the first place. For example, analysts who wanted to do "High Impact/Low Probability" Analysis would be led to question whether they have a sufficiently precisely described possibility whose consequences they are trying to discover. That is, they might realize that they need to back up and engage in the first two stages of counterfactual reasoning because they are not yet ready to engage in the third. Or, someone engaging in "What If" Analysis would be led to continue their analysis in a rigorous fashion beyond how their possibility might come to be in order to lead to (eventually) a full picture of the consequences of their possibility. In addition, an analyst can connect a "What If" Analysis on a subject to a "High Impact/Low Probability" Analysis. Thus, several new possibilities open for analysts when they recognize that these seemingly independent techniques are actually attempts to reproduce parts of a larger analytic process of counterfactual reasoning. Therefore, the prospects for using counterfactual reasoning, and how it might powerfully impact the analytic process, would seem to be very good.

To conclude this section, two further notes are worth mentioning for aficionados of these various techniques. The first concerns the way in which some of these techniques are often categorized. Sometimes, methods like "High Impact/Low Probability" Analysis and "What If" Analysis are termed "challenge" techniques, for they are (purportedly) designed to make analysts, strategists, and decision makers more open to other possibilities that they have not considered. This nicely maps back onto one of the secondary purposes of counterfactual reasoning: overcoming deterministic biases (like, in the case of these two techniques, foresight bias). However, if these techniques really turn out to be (as this section has argued) efforts at a part of counterfactual reasoning, then it would seem to be the case that they are not primarily "challenge" techniques at all. Instead, they are elements of the rational grounding of strategic assessment (as all counterfactual reasoning is). And, their benefits to overcoming biases (or opening up minds) would be a side

The *Prospects* for Counterfactual Reasoning
How it Can Replace Other Methods of Possibility Analysis

	Antecedent Scenario Selection	Intermediate State Selection	Consequent Scenario Selection
Subject of the Reasoning	*Origin* of the Possibility	*Orientation* of the Possibility	*Outcome* of the Possibility
Sequence of the Reasoning	How the Possibility *is Caused by* Other Events	How the Possibility *Coordinates with* Other Events	How the Possibility *Concludes in* Other Events
Superseded by the Reasoning	"What If" Analysis	"Scenario Fusion"	"High Impact/Low Probability," "Alternate Futures/Scenarios," "Red Team," & "Gaming" Analysis

Figure 3: Chart representing the potential for counterfactual reasoning to replace extant methods for assessing alternate possibilities (and what stage of counterfactual reasoning they map on to).

effect (or secondary matter). This suggests that, perhaps, the attempt to overcome bias should not be conceived of as an end in itself, but rather something that should result from the application of the appropriate reasoning techniques. Naturally, that suggestion takes things beyond the scope of this work, but it something this author offers to the reader for further reflection.

The second further note concerns the way in which retroactive assessments are typically left out of the analyst's typical set of structured methods. None of the usual methods are presented or taught (in general at least) as being applicable to the vital function of formulating "after-action" reports (i.e., retroactive assessments of strategy). But, counterfactual reasoning has as its most vital function the grounding of the underlying claims of strategic assessments both proactive (futures assessments) *and* retroactive (after-action reports). Therefore, by recognizing that these techniques are actually attempts at different pieces of an overall unified counterfactual reasoning process, they also can recognize the availability of them to a new family of problems that otherwise would seem to require a different (untaught) set of tools.

Chapter 6

Procedures of Counterfactual Reasoning Part 1: Antecedent Scenarios

A comprehensive system of counterfactual reasoning procedures (such as the one offered by this work) will be adequate to the extent that three criteria are satisfied. First, the procedures should exemplify the characteristics of all plausible reasoning principles. That is, they should possess clarity, precision, and consistency (both internally and externally with other well-established theories). Second, the procedures should be applicable to the real-life domain in which the reasoning is done. In this case, that means the realm of intelligence and security analysis, strategy, and decision making. Third, the procedures should yield the (known) correct results in the clear cases of that form of reasoning. Thus, a form of reasoning is "tested" (in part) by whether it is subject to "counterexamples" (i.e., instances in which the application of those principles would yield results that are counter to what is known to be the case). Obviously, there are always going to be controversial cases, and those make poor counterexamples. A plausible set of procedures should be helpful in controversial cases, but one should not reject a set of procedures because it does not produce the desired results in such instances.

The first two criteria exist in tension with each other. For, the domain of intelligence and security is fast-moving, and there is an upper bound on how precise any set of reasoning principles can be and still be applicable given the limits of time. On the other hand, the domain of intelligence and security also requires that one produce results that are sufficiently narrow to guide decision makers (i.e., are actionable). Thus, there is also a lower bound on how precise any set of reasoning principles can be. The ideal resolution of this tension (that the proposed model seeks to fulfill) is that *the maximum level of sophistication of the procedures is determined by what a well-educated analyst or strategist would be able to apply under normal circumstances, and the minimum level of sophistication of the procedures is determined by what a well-educated analyst or strategist would need in order to produce a definitive result that can guide decision makers*. As such, every effort has been made here to only provide the most relevant principles that are necessary (and sufficient) to yield clear (or as clear as it gets) results for analysts and strategists during the time period they are typically allotted. Thus, many nuances that apply only to fanciful (although still possible) cases have been left for another occasion. In addition, for the sake of space, this work does not offer a detailing of other rival assessments of these aspects of counterfactual reasoning and why they are mistaken. A litany of counterexamples to extant theories is also a matter for another occasion.[14]

The first proposed principle of counterfactual reasoning (from chapter 4) urged the centrality of structuring one's reasoning properly. The plausibility of a counterfactual product is extremely sensitive to how the reasoning that produced it was structured. As such, it is absolutely essential for analysts to keep their attention focused squarely on the two major problems of counterfactual reasoning. The first of these is the selection of antecedent scenarios. An antecedent scenario is the "back-story" of the possibility being assessed. It is how that possibility came to be. Thus, the selection of antecedent scenarios receives its own "stage" of counterfactual reasoning, is the subject of this section, and is part of the second principle of counterfactual reasoning.[15]

> **Counterfactual Reasoning Principle 2:** ***Any attempt to assess alternate possibilities, their consequences, and/or the relationships between them must begin by considering the antecedent scenario(s) that corresponds to the possibility in question.***

There might be cases in which assessment of possibilities starts out with an extremely detailed account of that possibility. In a case like that, the first stage may only amount to simply verifying that there already is an adequate antecedent scenario. However, *it is essential that analysts always start with antecedent scenarios, even if they think their possibility is already well understood.* For, more often than not, there are further details that need to be fleshed out. And many times, the "details" that are present are little more than assumptions that have yet to be subject to serious investigation.

The possibility that is the subject of the counterfactual reasoning (and whose consequences are the object of the inquiry) usually is only defined at the outset by a single statement. For example, one might be "Iran develops nuclear weapons technology" (a future alternative) or "The United States does not abolish the Iraqi army in 2003" (a past alternative). These brief statements usually serve as the "antecedent," or first part, of the counterfactual statement (what comes after the "if" but before the "then," as in "If X were to occur, then Y would occur"). The *antecedent scenario* represents the selected way in which that possibility came to be. There are (almost) always multiple possible ways for the antecedent to be (or have been) true. For a future alternative, this scenario begins at the present and charts a precise postulated future sequence of events that ends at the moment at which the antecedent would be true. For a past alternative, the scenario begins at the first place at which history is imagined to be different than it actually ways and then charts a precise sequence of events (which also change history) that ends at the moment at which the antecedent would be true.

A natural place to begin evaluation of antecedent scenarios would be with the generation of possible options. However, without sufficient guidance, it is all too easy for analysts to generate a series of options that are totally implausible or inapplicable to the challenge at hand. In many cases, there are an infinite number of possible antecedent scenarios that one could consider (most of which are completely implausible). Thus, possibilities should be generated with at least some sense of what the ultimate criteria are for assessing them.

Obviously, the ideal antecedent scenario would be the most plausible one. That is, it would be the most plausible way that the antecedent could (or could have) come to be. However, that advice means nothing without a clear definition of what plausibility entails. There must be a metric for measuring plausibility. There are two major candidates that appear in extant theories of counterfactuals. The most famous theory from philosophy (and logic) holds that counterfactuals are true based on what is true in the closest (i.e., most overall similar) possible world(s). Relative to selecting an antecedent scenario (or "point of deviation from the actual world") that similarity is measured primarily in terms of length of prior history that is perfectly preserved. That is, there is a preference for the shortest antecedent scenario (since it would preserve more prior history).[16] The other major theory from philosophy (and logic) holds that one should select the deviation from history (i.e., antecedent scenario) from the set that makes the antecedent most probable, the one that has the highest probability for its least probable event.[17] There is also a social scientific approach that incorporates both length of history and probability (although in slightly different ways). In that approach, a possibility is worth considering (i.e., it is a plausible antecedent scenario) based on not being too long (what is called the "minimal rewrite rule") and on the extent to which its initial event is probable (more precisely, there is a preference for reversing an improbable event rather than a more probable one).[18]

Without getting into the details of exactly what are the counter-examples to each of these approaches, suffice it to say that neither shortest length nor highest probability is individually (or collectively) necessary for a plausible antecedent scenario. And, the approaches of social scientists are not sufficient to yield an adequately precise result in many real-life cases. However, there are two elements from these theories that are important: the *temporal length of the scenario*, and the *probability of initial event in the scenario.*

In general, the shorter a scenario is, the better. If one can generate an antecedent by disrupting less history (or adding less, in the case of a future possibility), then it is better to do so (all things being equal). It is easy to see why this is the case, for the closer that history was (or is) temporally to a particular possibility coming-to-be, the more we would want to consider that possibility in our decision-making process. However, there are other factors. If a slightly longer scenario has a staring point (or *"triggering event"*) that is much more probable, that may make it more plausible. Often things are more probable in the long run than they are in the short run. And, that is important to keep in mind. One should not immediately pick the soonest case, since it may be far less probable than one that is a bit further off. Now, there is one more critical factor that has to be added in here. Scenarios can either spawn from a singular event that leads stepwise in sequence towards the antecedent, or distinct events that converge in order to produce the antecedent. Ultimately, while it is always possible for disparate events to conspire to bring about an outcome, more typically a small number of sequences will converge. As such, one has to consider the number of different chains of events that converge to yield the antecedent. That is, one must evaluate how many different changes have to be introduced to prior (or added to future) history *that are not attributable to prior changes that one has already made.* All other things being equal, the fewer such sequences, the better. A more unified scenario is preferred. Therefore, there are three major elements that have to be considered in antecedent scenarios: *temporal length*, *triggering event probability*, and *unity*.

A reasonable generation of possible antecedent scenarios for consideration would take these three elements into consideration.

> **Counterfactual Reasoning Principle 3:** ***Possible antecedent scenarios should be generated with imagination and openness to many options, but with some preference for those that are shorter in temporal length, higher in triggering event probability, and higher in unity.***

This principle does not ask analysts and strategists to fully weigh these three factors, only to use them to guide the generation process (and weed out the truly fanciful possibilities). Another principle to narrow down the range of options to consider would be:

> **Counterfactual Reasoning Principle 4:** ***Possible antecedent scenarios should be eliminated if they require either a violation of a well-established law of nature or an event that is extremely highly improbable (given all events immediately prior to it).***

Thus, a scenario that would violate the known laws of physics should be removed from consideration. (Note: the "laws of nature" does not here mean mere statistical generalizations, etc., but things that, if they occurred, a rational person would be inclined to term them a literal "miracle.") In addition, a scenario that includes one or more extremely highly improbable events should also be excluded. (Note: probability in "extremely highly improbable" is assessed in terms of all events prior to the events occurrence. The assessment is not made only with events that occur years or months earlier, but in terms of the complete history.) In addition, this assessment is relative to the other options. It might be that the antecedent simply requires things that are very highly improbable. In that case, this principle would simply urge that one eliminate the most improbable from those options.[19]

Once the antecedent scenarios for consideration are generated, they are assessed relative to each other. That is, one ranks each in terms of three "elements of plausibility": its *temporal length* (how long it takes to get to the antecedent being true from the initial deviation/triggering event from actual history), *triggering event probability* (how probable the initial deviation/triggering event is, given the events prior to it), and *unity* (how many initial deviations/triggering events and resulting sequences of events converge to generate the antecedent).

> **Counterfactual Reasoning Principle 5:** ***Possible antecedent scenarios should be ranked (relative to each other) in terms of their temporal length, triggering event probability, and unity.***

In this ranking, it is possible (albeit uncommon in the case of length) for two (or more scenarios) to be tied.

In comparing two antecedent scenarios, if one of those two scenarios is superior to the other in terms of more of these three elements (than the other scenario is superior to it), then that scenario is more plausible.

> **Counterfactual Reasoning Principle 6:** ***If antecedent scenario S1 is superior to antecedent scenario S2 in more elements of plausibility that S2 is superior than S1, then S1 is more plausible than S2 (and is more reasonable to select than S2).***

Note that there are *four* ways that principle 6 could be satisfied: 1) S1 is better than S2 in terms of all 3 elements of plausibility, 2) S1 is better than S2 in terms of 2 elements of plausibility, and S1 and S2 are tied in terms of the third element of plausibility, 3) S1 is better than S2 in terms of 2 elements of plausibility, and S2 is better than S1 in terms of the third element of plausibility, and 4) S1 is better than S2 in terms of one of the elements of plausibility, and S1 and S2 are tied in terms of the other 2 elements of plausibility. For most comparisons, principle 6 will be satisfied in one of these ways, and so one of the scenarios will be shown to be more plausible. Successive applications of this principle to other scenarios would then ultimately yield the most plausible scenario, which is then affirmed to be the antecedent scenario.

If principle 6 does not produce a preference between two possible antecedent scenarios, it is possible that there is a tie (more on that in a moment). But, there is one way to break ties in some cases:

Counterfactual Reasoning Principle 7: ***If antecedent scenario S1 is superior to antecedent scenario S2 in one element of plausibility, and S2 is superior to S1 in terms of one element of plausibility, and S1 and S2 are tied in terms of one element of plausibility, but S1 has a greater degree of superiority to S2 (in the relevant element) than S2 has to S1 (in the relevant element), then S1 is more plausible than S2 (and is more reasonable to select than S2).***

This sort of situation is not especially common, but it is worth noting.

A pure tie among antecedent scenarios is rare, but in the case that it does occur, there are two options. In terms of antecedent scenario plausibility, there is no way to distinguish between the two cases. But, it is possible to either 1) go ahead and use both antecedent scenarios and only accept intermediate states and consequent scenarios that work with both scenarios, or 2) go back and modify the original antecedent to specify one of the antecedent scenarios over the others. This latter possibility leads to a final principle for antecedent scenario selection.

Counterfactual Reasoning Principle 8: ***After selecting an antecedent scenario, verify that the scenario captures the intention that was behind the consideration of the possibility in the first place.***

There could be instances in which, upon further reflection, it is clear that the analyst (or customer) really has a much more specific possibility in mind. Or, it could be that the antecedent scenario is, for some other reason, clearly not the most appropriate one to consider. In general, analysts should accept a surprising result from principles 2–7, but there could be instances where the result (interesting though it may be) is just not what needs to be analyzed in this case. If that happens, then one has to backtrack and restart the process. But, as in most cases, if the antecedent scenario is adequate, then one may continue on to addressing the next major challenge of counterfactual reason in the second stage.

Chapter 7

Procedures of Counterfactual Reasoning
Part 2: Intermediate States

Well-justified counterfactual conclusions derive from well-structured counterfactual reasoning. An essential element of that structure is sharp focus on the two major challenges of counterfactual reasoning, which are also the subject of the first two stages of counterfactual reasoning. The second of these stages is *intermediate state selection*.

The antecedent scenario ends as soon as the conditions obtain sufficient to make the antecedent true. Yet the time of interest to the analyst or strategist (i.e., the time of the consequents they are considering) is often much later. Thus, the period that begins immediately after the antecedent scenario ends and that extends until the time of interest to the analyst (for the potential consequent of the counterfactual) is populated by "intermediate states." These intermediate states are events that either actually occurred during that time (if a past alternate possibility is being considered) or are independently projected to occur during that time (if a future alternate possibility is being considered).

In a sense, intermediate states are already known to the analyst. They are *not* something that the analyst has to come up with (with one exception noted at the end). Instead, the analyst has to determine not *what* they are, but *whether they are reasonable to include* in the period between the antecedent and the consequent scenario. These events occurred (or were projected to occur) based upon a different set of events than those in the antecedent scenario. As such, they might play out differently if the antecedent scenario were to occur (or have occurred). *That* is the analyst's task: determine which states are plausibly held still to occur even with the changes that come from postulating the antecedent scenario.

To begin assessing intermediate states, the analyst or strategist must identify the complete sequence of events that did occur (or is independently projected to occur) after the antecedent scenario ends but before the consequent scenario begins *and the probability of each of those events.*

Counterfactual Reasoning Principle 9: ***Possible intermediate states should be generated by identifying the sequence(s) of events that occurred (or are projected to occur) between the antecedent scenario and the consequent scenario as well as the probability of each of those events.***

Each possible intermediate state will have an "original probability." In the case of a past alternate possibility, this will be the probability of that event *given what actually happened instead of the events of the antecedent scenario.* In the case of a future alternate possibility, this will be the probability of that event *given what is true of the world now.* Ultimately, intermediate states are selected based upon a comparison of their original probability and their probability *given the assumption of the antecedent scenario AND all other prior intermediate states.* The assessment of intermediate states must proceed in *temporal order* (not in order of subject matter). This is because any event that is determined to be an intermediate state will become part of what is used to assess any other (later) possible intermediate states. Hence, the background that is used to evaluate possible intermediate states is constantly changing as more events are established to be intermediate states.

Counterfactual Reasoning Principle 10: ***Possible intermediate states should be assessed in order of the time at which they occurred (or are projected to occur) and by means of comparing their original probability to their probability given the antecedent scenario and any prior intermediate states.***

There are four different ways that an event can qualify as an intermediate state. And the next three principles identify three of those possibilities.

Counterfactual Reasoning Principle 11: ***If a possible intermediate state's probability given the antecedent scenario (and any prior intermediate states) is exactly the same as its original probability, then it is reasonable to include as an intermediate state.***

Counterfactual Reasoning Principle 12: ***If a possible intermediate state's probability given the antecedent scenario (and any prior intermediate states) is exactly greater than its original probability, then it is reasonable to include as an intermediate state.***

> **Counterfactual Reasoning Principle 13:** ***If a possible intermediate state's probability given the antecedent scenario (and any prior intermediate states) is not exactly greater and not exactly the same as its original probability, but still sufficiently high, then it is reasonable to include as an intermediate state.***

Roughly speaking, there are several possible results that can arise from comparing a possible event's original probability to its probability given the antecedent scenario (and any prior intermediate states): greater, lesser, or equal. Unfortunately, none of those are what principles 11–13 refer to, *strictly speaking*. An event could have the same numerical probability, given the antecedent scenario that it had originally, and yet still have been affected by events in that scenario (i.e., it is both increased and decreased in a way that equaled out in the end). Thus, "exactly the same" means that none of the events in the antecedent scenario (and prior intermediate states) had any affect on the probability of the possible intermediate state.[20] In a similar way, "exactly greater" means that none of the events in the antecedent scenario (and prior intermediate states) had any effect on the probability of the possible intermediate state *other than a positive one*. Thus, "not exactly greater and not exactly the same" means that the events of the antecedent scenario (and prior intermediate states) had either only a negative effect or an at least temporary negative effect on the probability of the possible intermediate state.

If a possible intermediate state's probability is unaffected or only increased by the antecedent scenario (and prior intermediate states), then that event is reasonably admitted. But, even if it is affected partially (or only) in a negative way, it still may turn out to be admissible *if the probability is still sufficiently high.* If a future event was reasonable to project, then it had a reasonably high probability; and if that probability is still reasonably high, even given the changes postulated in the antecedent scenario, there is no reason not to still project that the event will occur. In a similar fashion, if a prior event was very probable, and is still very probable even if the antecedent scenario had occurred, there is no reason to think that it would not have occurred. It is still reasonable to affirm it (after all, it is still very probable). Now, there is no particular threshold offered here as to what is "sufficiently high." Presumably it will (at least) be higher than 0.50. But, some may prefer a more robust amount.

Ultimately, this approach to intermediate state selection is more conservative than the most popular approach, and more liberal than the major rival of that approach. According to the popular "similarity" approach to counterfactuals, an actual event will also hold in the counterfactual scenario if it holds in the closest possible world(s). Thus, in many cases, any event that is even consistent with the antecedent will still be affirmed (even if its probability is significantly lowered by the antecedent scenario, or is partially lowered but is not very high at the end).[21] By contrast, the rival "probability" approach (that emphasizes the probability of the event given the antecedent scenario) would include the event only if its probability is unaffected or only increased by the antecedent scenario.[22] This approach, in marked contrast, does not admit events whose probability is low given the antecedent scenario (contra "similarity" theory), but does admit events whose probability is high given the antecedent scenario, even if it was in some manner affected by the antecedent scenario (contra "probability" theory).

There is one final way that an event can be admitted as an intermediate state: if it is itself justifiable as the consequent of a counterfactual with the same antecedent (and antecedent scenario) as the one under consideration (i.e., it is part of a "supporting counterfactual"). In other words, an event might not qualify under principles 11–13, but satisfy the criteria set forth in section 8 for being part of the consequent scenario of a counterfactual with a shorter intermediate period.

> **Counterfactual Reasoning Principle 14:** ***If a possible intermediate state could qualify as part of a consequent scenario of a counterfactual with the same antecedent (and antecedent scenario) as the one under consideration (it is part of a reasonable "supporting counterfactual"), then it is reasonable to include as an intermediate state.***

Thus, after trying to apply principles 11–13, one should proceed to the see whether the state can satisfy any of the principles in the next section. If it does, then that event is admitted as an intermediate state. (Note: The supporting counterfactual must feature a "would" as its modal connection and not merely a "might.") If not, then the next state should be assessed, and so on.

In looking for possible supporting counterfactuals (and only at this point), one should consider events that did not occur (for a past alternative) or that are not already projected to occur (for a future alternative). After all, the antecedent scenario is a change that might not only stop events from happening that did (or might) occur without it. That change could also result in new events that otherwise would (or might) not occur at all. Therefore, we arrive at the final principle for evaluating possible intermediate states:

> **Counterfactual Reasoning Principle 15:** ***In assessing possible events that would be part of a supporting counterfactual, one should consider events that did not occur (or were not projected to occur) without the antecedent scenario.***

Chapter 8

Procedures of Counterfactual Reasoning Part 3: Consequent Scenarios

The uninitiated counterfactual reasoner is likely to attempt immediately to assess the possible outcomes of their "what if" situation. This work has emphasized the importance of resisting that temptation. Instead, appropriate counterfactual reasoning first directly engages the two major challenges of counterfactual reasoning and its first two stages, which concern antecedent scenarios and intermediate states. However, while these first two stages deserve emphasis, because it is so intuitively attractive to neglect them, that does not mean there are not important issues surrounding the selection of consequent scenarios.

The distinction between what is approached as a possible intermediate state and what is approached as a possible (part of a) consequent scenario ultimately depends on the intentions of the analyst or strategist. Strictly speaking, the consequent scenario is simply the way in which the consequent of the counterfactual is true, and the immediate aftermath of the consequent. As such, its scope is determined by the range of time of interest for the counterfactual inquiry. For example, in the case of the 10 year consequences of a nuclear-armed Iran, the consequent scenario is made up by the events of that tenth year, and the intermediate states are all that occurs during the years prior to that (but after the full acquisition of nuclear weapons). Thus, the analyst or strategist could just as easily have considered the 9 year consequences, in which case, the events of the ninth year would not be potential intermediate states, but a consequent scenario. (This is the reason for principle 14. A counterfactual with an earlier consequent scenario can provide intermediate states for counterfactuals with the same antecedent scenario and a later time for their consequent scenario). Thus, ultimately, the analyst or strategist will have some sort of timeframe in mind when they come to the second and third stages of counterfactual reasoning. And once they have filled up the period prior to that time with intermediate states, they then shift to consideration of the consequent scenarios.

The extant approaches to counterfactual reasoning are fairly unanimous in terms of their accounts of how to select consequent scenarios. They hold that a particular event is part of what *would* occur in a consequent scenario if and only if it occurs in *every* conceivable circumstance (i.e., "possible world") that is consistent with (i.e., does not contradict) the events of the antecedent scenario and intermediate states. And, they hold that a particular event is part of what *might* occur in a consequent scenario if and only if it occurs in *at least one* conceivable circumstance that is consistent with the events of the antecedent scenario and intermediate states.[23] Or, to put the matter another way, an event *would* occur in the consequent scenario if and only if its probability given the antecedent scenario and intermediate states is 1.00, and an event *might* occur in the consequent scenario if and only if its probability given the antecedent scenario and intermediate states is greater than 0.

Despite this widespread agreement among extant theories of how to understand the meaning of "would" and "might," this approach is simply inadequate for intelligence and national security. There are simply too few options that would have a probability of 1.00, and too many that would have a probability greater than 0. This approach would render counterfactual reasoning rather unhelpful in grounding strategy assessments. One would invariably end up claiming that not much of anything (of interest) would happen (for sure), and with the obligation to say that almost everything might happen (in some situations). But, one hardly needs to go through the mechanics of counterfactual reasoning (or any other cognitive method) to come up with such placid claims. Now, despite this rather harsh assessment, there are two things of benefit that could come from this approach. First, while few things of interest are likely to be such that they would happen, some things of interest might be such that they would *not* happen. Second, among the large number of things that would likely be such that they might happen, some might turn out to have been previously unforeseen by the analyst or strategist. Thus, this approach is not entirely without practical use. It is simply not enough, however, to be what this work recommends.

The primary reason that extant approaches to counterfactual reasoning (especially from philosophy and logic) end up with this theory of rather limited application to real-life cases is that this is not their primary objective. Instead, their goal is to show how counterfactuals could be true or false, and not how one would go about reasoning through such counterfactuals in a real-life situation. By contrast, this work's paradigm for counterfactual reasoning is primarily motivated by the desire to construct a prescriptive theory of counterfactual reasoning: a way to determine whether specific counterfactual claims can reasonably be believed to be true or false (with a particular focus on grounding strategic assessment).

Since the most fundamental purpose of counterfactual reasoning in analysis and strategy is to ground the statements necessary to do strategic assessment (whether proactive or retroactive), this approach offers a radical new interpretation of how to select consequent scenarios. *Consequent scenarios are selected on the basis of what would be useful to set up full-fledged strategic assessments.* That is, if counterfactual claims are so vital to analysis and strategy because they are universal underpinnings of strategic assessment, then the model of counterfactual reasoning has to yield claims that are usable for strategic assessment. And, in order to do strategic assessment of various possible decisions or situations and their consequences, there are three major things that are needed. First, one has to know what sorts of consequences are worth thinking about in the decision-making process (these are consequents of a counterfactual). Second, one has to know what decisions or situations the outcomes are related to (these are the antecedents of a counterfactual). And then, one needs to know the nature of the connection between the decision or situation and the particular consequence (this is the modal connection of the counterfactual).

It is fairly clear how to derive the first element. The antecedent is clarified in developing the antecedent scenario. The second two elements are determined together. For, an event serves as a consequent insofar as there is an appropriate modal connection between it and the antecedent (and vice versa). And, there are two modal connections: "would" and "might." It seems clear that a probability of 1.00 is too strong for "would," and a probability of more than 0 is too weak for "might." Instead, this work proposes that these two modalities be interpreted instead as *indicating that a consequence is worthy of consideration using the principles of decision making under risk ("would") or the principles of decision making under uncertainty ("might").* These two forms of strategic assessment are the dominant paradigms of rational decision making. For cases of decisions whose possible consequences have a known (or ascertainable) probability, one applies the principles of decision making under risk (i.e., decision theory "proper").[24] For cases of decisions whose possible consequences do not have a known (or ascertainable) probability, one applies the principles of decision making under uncertainty (i.e., game theory, etc.)[25] Thus, ultimately, counterfactual reasoning has to deliver claims that are reasonable and suitable for one of these two forms of strategic assessment.

On this "strategic" theory of consequent scenario selection, the terms "would" and "might" *per se* are actually discarded as not especially useful. Instead, they are replaced with (or reinterpreted as): "has a nonzero and ascertainable probability of occurring" ("would") and "has a nonzero (even if otherwise not ascertainable) probability of occurring" ("might"). A set of possible decisions whose consequences have a nonzero and ascertainable probability of occurring are reasonably assessed using the principles of decision making under risk. A set of possible decisions whose consequences have a nonzero (even if otherwise not ascertainable) probability of occurring are reasonably assessed using the principles of decision making under uncertainty. Thus, this approach to consequent scenario selection offers the analyst and strategist what they need from counterfactual reasoning (a reasonable grounding for strategic assessments). In addition, it directly urges them to go on and use the appropriate principles for strategic assessment (either under risk or under uncertainty).[26]

The process of consequent scenario selection begins by identifying all the events that are possibly part of a consequent scenario.

> **Counterfactual Reasoning Principle 16:** ***Possible consequent scenarios should be generated by identifying all the sequences of events that are consistent with (i.e., do not contradict) the events of the intermediate states, antecedent scenarios, and history prior to that.***

In general, one should anticipate that *there are going to be multiple consequent scenarios.* However, one should still attempt to identify anything that is common to all sequences of events generated by principle 16. To do this, one attempts to see in what proportion of the generated sequences does a particular event occur (or not occur).

Counterfactual Reasoning Principle 17: ***Possible consequent scenarios should be assessed by identifying how frequently (or in what proportion) a particular event occurs in all the sequences of events that are consistent with (i.e., do not contradict) the events of the intermediate states, antecedent scenarios, and history prior to that.***

Counterfactual Reasoning Principle 18: ***Possible consequent scenarios should be selected by first looking for events (of interest) that do not occur in any of the sequences of events that are consistent with (i.e., do not contradict) the events of the intermediate states, antecedent scenarios, and history prior to that. The nonoccurrence of any such events will be part of all consequent scenarios.***

The most critical question for selecting consequent scenarios (beyond identifying events that occur in at least one sequence consistent with prior history) is whether that event has a probability that is ascertainable or not. Any event that has a nonzero probability (i.e., occurs in at least one sequence consistent with the prior history) will be worthy of consideration as a consequence in decision making under uncertainty (i.e., it "might" happen, in the relevant sense).

Counterfactual Reasoning Principle 19: ***If an event has a nontrivial nonzero probability of occurring, given the events of the intermediate states, antecedent scenarios, and history prior to that, then that event is reasonable to accept as part of a consequent scenario that might occur (and hence be considered as a consequence in decision making under uncertainty). This is true even if that event's probability is otherwise not ascertainable.***

To say that an event has a "nontrivial" probability of occurring is a somewhat relative assessment. It means that if one is making a list of consequent scenarios, and that list appears to be large, and some of the scenarios clearly are very highly improbable, those need not be considered. By contrast, if there are fewer possible consequent scenarios, one of those might be worth considering. That is, there is a limit to the number of consequences one can reasonably consider in decision making under uncertainty. So, a probability will be trivial relative to the number and nature of the other options.

Any event that has a nonzero and ascertainable probability will be worthy of consideration as a consequence in decision making under risk (i.e., it "would" happen, in the relevant sense).

> **Counterfactual Reasoning Principle 20:** ***If an event has a nonzero and ascertainable probability of occurring given the events of the intermediate states, antecedent scenarios, and history prior to that, then that event is reasonable to accept as part of a consequent scenario that would occur (and hence be considered as a consequence in decision making under risk).***

Two important qualifications need to be made at this point. First, the fact that something would happen implies that it might happen (but not necessarily vice versa, of course). Thus, one should not automatically assume that because something can be assessed strategically in terms of decision making under risk it cannot also be assessed in terms of decision making under uncertainty. In fact, anything that is assessable in terms of the former can also be assessable (at least in principle) in terms of the latter. Ultimately, the decision of which set of principles to use in a case like that is a subject for strategy assessment, not counterfactual reasoning. What counterfactual reasoning provides is the underpinnings that make one or more possible, not the basis to determine which should be used.

A second qualification concerns the way in which one determines if something has an ascertainable probability. This *is not a matter of whether it can be estimated.* For, one can always come up with some sort of estimate if one is willing to be sufficiently "rough" in the estimate. Thus, the issue is more *the extent to which that estimate is a reasonably well-supported one.* And that is ultimately a question of how much of a statistical generalization can be made about what occurs in all the sequences of events that are consistent with the antecedent scenario, intermediate states, and prior history before that.[77] If numbers can reasonably be inferred, then the probability is "ascertainable" in the relevant sense. But, if they are only very rough estimates at best, then they the probability is not "ascertainable."

Chapter 9

Practices of Counterfactual Reasoning

The most central proposal of this work is that counterfactual reasoning constitutes an essential component of analysis and strategy. This proposal is based upon three supporting proposals (each of which is able to justify the central proposal on their own). First, the *Strategic Presumption of Counterfactuals* recognizes that all strategies (and analyses of them) are grounded in a series of counterfactual claims about alternate possibilities, their consequences, and the relationships between them. That is, well-justified strategy assessment requires well-justified underlying counterfactual claims. And well-justified counterfactual claims can be achieved by means of following the twenty principles of counterfactual reasoning described in the previous sections of this work. This is the first reason why counterfactual reasoning is essential to analysis and strategy.

The *Systematic Potential of Counterfactuals* urged that extant methods for assessing alternate possibilities, their consequences, and the relationships between them (such as "What If" Analysis, "High Impact/Low Probability" Analysis, etc.) are ultimately not distinct from, but are different aspects of, a single process: counterfactual reasoning. Not only does counterfactual reasoning serve to ground major claims underlying strategic assessment, but it can unify (or replace) a diverse series of extant methods for evaluating possibilities with a comprehensive system. This is the second reason why counterfactual reasoning is essential to analysis and strategy.

All that remains, then, is the third (and boldest) major proposal:

> **Third Major Proposal (The Structural Priority of Counterfactuals):** ***All assessment of alternate possibilities, their consequences, and the relationships between them should ultimately be conditional (as it is in counterfactual reasoning).***

Once again, one should note that all the rest of this work stands independent of this third proposal. Thus, even if the argument that follows is mistaken, the prior sections of this work still emerge unscathed. In this final section, reasons will be offered for thinking that all assessment of alternate possibilities should be done conditionally (i.e., in terms of what would or might happen if a specific possibility were to occur).

There are two major contexts in which alternate possibilities are assessed (and that have been mentioned throughout this work). The first is retroactive possibility assessment (how things could have been different in the past). This is the object of "after-action" analysis: what would or might have happened if things had been done differently. The second is proactive possibility assessment (how things could be in the future). This is the object of "futures analysis": what will or might happen in the future.

It is fairly easy to show that retroactive possibility assessment should be conditional. In that case, there simply is no alternative. To assess the decisions of the past, one cannot simply consider what did occur as a result of the actual decision. For the fact that a good outcome came about does not mean the decision was reasonable, and the fact that a bad outcome came about does not mean the decision was unreasonable. Instead, one has to consider what would or might have occurred if other decisions had been made instead. Apart from such analysis, "reasonable decision making" becomes indistinguishable from "luck." There has to be a way to separate cases of good outcomes due to a fortunate turn of events from good outcomes that result from reasonable decisions. Only a conditional approach allows that. Thus, fairly clearly, retroactive possibility assessment should be conditional (as it is on counterfactual reasoning).

The real issue is whether proactive possibility assessment, such as futures analysis, needs to be conditional. In general, most theorists deny that it has to be so. The two primary approaches to futures analysis are both categorical. That is, they seek a nonconditional claim as their ultimate conclusion, such as "Y will (probably/plausibly) occur," instead of "If X were to occur, then Y would (or might) occur." The first approach is "forecasting." In this approach, a single variable (or set of variables) is extrapolated forward according to probabilistic models that presume a defined rate of change or continuation of a particular trend. The result is a single estimate of that variable (or variables). Or, in some approaches, a hierarchy of possible estimates is the result. The second approach is "futuring." In this approach, a set of "drivers" is selected in terms of which is most uncertain and relevant to a particular kind of outcome. Then, the technique explores the ways in which those drivers could evolve in terms of different potential scenarios (ways things might go).[28]

There are a number of problems with futures analysis as practiced under these two extant approaches (that are nonconditional). First, there is always a very restricted amount of information that can be employed in futures analysis. Regardless of how advanced one's technological tools for collection, and how ingenious one's sources may be, one can only use events in the past or present to do analysis of the future in these approaches. This is a fundamental structural point that simply cannot be avoided in these approaches. Second, there is a limit to how much rigorous analysis can be done with these two methods. Forecasting applies (typically) to a very limited range of highly quantifiable cases. And futuring is reasonably low in terms of the specific guiding principles that can be offered on how to formulate and evaluate scenarios. So, while these two approaches offer more rigor than no structured method at all, the degree of rigor is fairly modest.

These two combine to generate two further problems for futures analysis that are much more pernicious. The third problem is a significantly increased potential for bias in futures analysis. There is a general paucity of information and reasoning methods available for futures analysis. And, *whenever the availability of reasoning methods and reliable information is at is minimum, the attractiveness of biases is at its maximum.* Analysts and strategists do not seek to be biased. Instead, they end up biased due to their choices, capabilities, and circumstances. When a determination has to be made, and the information and methods are insufficient to guide towards one answer, the mind will invariably find a way to formulate a judgment. And that will have to be based on some sort of nonrational factor (since the rational ones will have been inadequate). Fourth, there is a significantly decreased specificity in futures analysis. Restricted information and reasoning methods means that one has to be much more general in the conclusions that one makes (even if one manages to avoid biases). And the more general the conclusions of futures analysis, the less useful that they will be to the ultimate decision makers. Greater event-specificity is essential to the most useful strategy and decision making.

A third approach to futures analysis that avoids all four of these problems (at least to a much greater extent than the extant approaches) is possible. This approach is the "conditional/counterfactual" approach. In this approach, *the only judgments about the future that are made are those that are conditional/counterfactual: statements about what would or might occur if a particular event were to occur.* No statements (in general at least) would be made that some event simply will or might occur (without conditioning on some other future event's occurrence). On this view, futures assessment is always done in terms of counterfactual reasoning.

There are four advantages to this approach (which are each a reversal of the four problems of extant approaches to futures analysis). First, there are fewer restrictions on the information one can employ in assessing the future. There is a way to use more than just past and present events in analyzing the future. *One can use future events if one approaches them conditionally/counterfactually* (i.e., IF this future event were to occur, THEN…). This provides a much larger range of possible information to use in assessing the future. For now, the future may be used to analyze itself.

Second, there is a much more rigorous set of principles that can employed in the method itself in assessing the future. The model of counterfactual reasoning that this work proposes (as exemplified by the twenty principles) provides a fairly detailed list of instructions for how to assess such possibilities. It is always possible to introduce further principles (this is a *basic* guide after all). But, these twenty principles are a substantial guide to analysts and strategists that goes well beyond what is typically available under the extant approaches (in at least most cases).

Third, there is a reduced temptation towards bias in assessing the future. There are two reasons for this. First, one has removed (or at least decreased) the two reasons that encourage bias in the extant approaches. One has increased the available information and rigorousness of the methods. Second, one forces the analysts to state their assumptions much more emphatically. In futuring, for example, the selection of the "drivers" that generate the scenarios is, by far, the most vital task. In many ways, the selection of drivers, in itself, determines the outcome of the analysis. But there is not any especially rigorous or principle-based way to do this. By contrast, on the conditional/counterfactual approach, one is forced to put one's assumption to the forefront and flat out state that thus-and-so would or might occur *if X were to occur*. Thus, even if one has some irrational affinity to, or fascination with, X, one has stated fairly clearly that one's conclusion only holds if X were to occur. The analysts and their consumer are forced to recognize the conditional/counterfactual nature of the claim. Thus, it brings intellectual modesty (or at least transparency) to the forefront.

Fourth, there is a much greater potential for event-specificity in assessing the future. Once one introduces the possibility of conditionalizing on a very precise set of potential future events, the possibility emerges of a much more precise set of consequences of (and strategies for responding to) those events. Ultimately, strategy has to be precise, one has to set out a significant amount of detail in terms of many different elements, and that is far easier to do if one has greater detail in the specificity of the events. That is possible on the conditional/counterfactual approach.

The *Practices* of Counterfactual Reasoning

Three Approaches to Proactive Possibility Assessment (e.g. Futures Analysis)

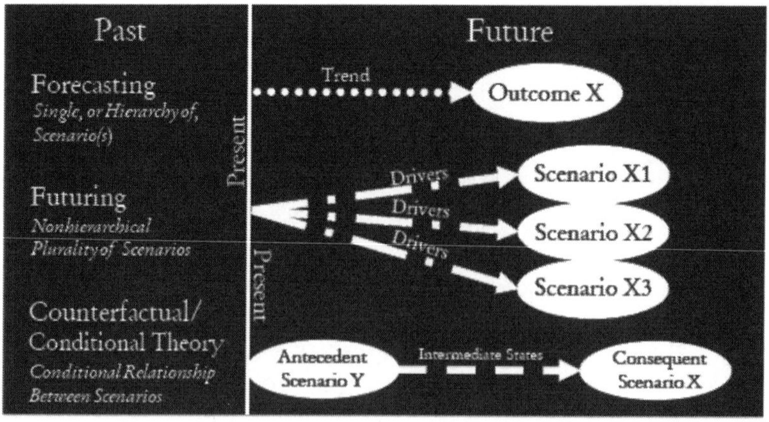

Figure 4: Chart representing the three approaches to future analysis and how the counterfactual reasoning approach differs from the two extant approaches (forecasting and futuring).

The conditional/counterfactual approach to futures analysis has four major advantages over both of the extant (categorical) approaches. There is reason to think that counterfactual reasoning is not only a way to do analysis of future possibilities, but that it is (perhaps) the best (or only appropriate) way to do proactive analysis of alternate possibilities. Since it is clear that it is also the best (or only appropriate) way to do retroactive analysis of alternate possibilities, it is reasonable to conclude that *The Structural Priority of Counterfactuals* is true. All assessment of alternate possibilities should be done conditionally (as it is with counterfactual reasoning). This is the third argument that counterfactual reasoning is essential to analysis and strategy.

Chapter 10

Pitfalls of Counterfactual Reasoning

Suppose that an analyst employs all the principles described in this work and concludes that the following two counterfactuals are true:

CF1. If Iran were to develop nuclear weapons, then Hezbollah would be able to acquire nuclear weapons.

CF2. If Hezbollah were able to acquire nuclear weapons, then Israel would be attacked by nuclear weapons.

Now suppose that the analyst notices that the consequent of CF1 has the same possibility as the antecedent of CF2 (i.e., "Hezbollah is able to acquire nuclear weapons"). The analyst thereby concludes that the following counterfactual is true:

CF3. If Iran were to develop nuclear weapons, then Israel would be attacked by nuclear weapons.

In this case, the analyst is not employing any of the twenty principles of counterfactual reasoning that have been described in this work. For, there are two ways to reason counterfactually. The first (and most basic) is to infer a counterfactual from other statements that are not themselves counterfactuals (as in all the discussion of counterfactual reasoning thus far). This is the most fundamental kind of counterfactual reasoning. The second is to infer a counterfactual from another counterfactual (as in the above inference). A small piece of this has already been seen in the way that supporting counterfactuals can be used to provide intermediate states for other counterfactuals. But, in those cases, one would ultimately be inferring one counterfactual based on another counterfactual *and* many other statements that are not counterfactuals. Up until now, there has been no discussion of how one might reason only from one or more counterfactual statements to another counterfactual statement.

The most basic counterfactual reasoning task for analysts is to show what counterfactuals are true based upon other kinds of claims that are not themselves counterfactuals. To reason from one counterfactual to another is a more advanced counterfactual reasoning task. And since this work is designed to provide the *basic* guidelines for counterfactual reasoning, this topic goes well beyond the scope of this work. For ultimately, only a formalized system of counterfactual logic would provide the complete account of how to reason from one counterfactual to another.[29] However, there are a few major points that can (and should) be made here. In particular, there are three major ways to reason from one counterfactual to another that are extremely tempting but are *invalid.* That is, they involve reasoning in such a way that the premises do not support the conclusion (even though they may seem to do so). They are three major counterfactual *fallacies,* and every counterfactual reasoner should be careful to avoid all of three.

The first fallacy is *counterfactual transitivity.* Consider Reinhard Gehlen, a leader in the Nazi Eastern Front intelligence operations, who was later recruited to work in a West German anti-Soviet intelligence organization and aid NATO operations after World War II (WWII). An example of employing counterfactual transitivity with inferences about him might run as follows:

CF4. If Reinhard Gehlen had not been a Nazi, then he would not have been involved in leading Nazi intelligence operations on the Eastern front.

CF5. If Reinhard Gehlen had not been involved in leading Nazi intelligence operations on the Eastern front, then he would not have been a supporter of NATO operations after WWII.

Therefore…

CF6. If Reinhard Gehlen had not been a Nazi, then he would not have been a supporter of NATO operations after WW2.

This inference is a very tempting one, since the possibility imagined in the consequent of CF4 is the same as the possibility imagined in the antecedent of CF5 (namely, Gehlen not being involved in leading Nazi intelligence operations on the Eastern Front). Thus, it seems natural to connect the possibility of the antecedent of CF4 with the possibility of the consequent of CF5. This is even more attractive because it is plainly a valid inference with conditionals that are *not counterfactuals.* For example:

NCF1. If Reinhard Gehlen is a Nazi, then Reinhard Gehlen is pro-WWII Germany.

NCF2. If Reinhard Gehlen is pro-WWII Germany, then Reinhard Gehlen is anti-USSR.

Therefore…

NCF3. If Reinhard Gehlen is a Nazi, then Reinhard Gehlen is anti-USSR.

The inference from NCF1 and NCF2 to NCF3 is a valid one. That is, if NCF1 and NCF2 are true, then NCF3 must also be true. This is sometimes termed "conditional transitivity," or "hypothetical inference," and it is one of the most basic kinds of valid reasoning. However, the fact that this works with standard conditionals does not imply that it works with counterfactuals. Counterfactuals are a special kind of conditional, and they follow their own set of unique rules. Therefore, the kinds of reasoning one can do with other conditionals does not automatically apply to counterfactuals. This is a major example of that.

To show that counterfactual transitivity is a fallacy requires that one have an example where the premises are true (e.g., CF4 and CF5) but the conclusion could be false (CF6). The possibility of true premises and a false conclusion is sufficient to show that a type of reasoning is *invalid.* And that is clearly possible with this example. CF4 seems entirely plausible. Non-Nazis do not get to be involved in leading Nazi intelligence operations on the Eastern Front. And CF5 also seems true, for if Gehlen did not have the job that he did, then he would likely have been either a) killed in battle, b) not recruited by the West, but tried for war crimes, or c) not recruited by the West and sent home as a bitter ex-Nazi. In all cases, he would not have ended up as a supporter of NATO operations after WWII. Despite this, it is entirely plausible that CF6 is false. For, if Gehlen had not been a Nazi, he could still easily have been a supporter of NATO operations after WW2. Thus, the truth of CF4 and CF5 does not guarantee that CF6 is true.

More generally, the following form of reasoning is a counterfactual fallacy:

Fallacy of Counterfactual Transitivity;

1. If it were the case that X, then it would be the case that Y.
2. If it were the case that Y, then it would be the case that Z.

   Do not automatically imply that,

3. If it were the case that X, then it would be the case that Z.

This does not mean that "3" is false, but only that "1" and "2" are not sufficient to show that "3" is true. Thus, if one were going to show that "3" is true, one would have to do so in a different way.[30]

The reason that this proves to be a fallacy is that it is possible that the antecedent scenario for X and the antecedent scenario for Y are very different. And that difference could have an impact on whether Z is plausible. In the case of Gehlen, the antecedent scenario for X (he is not a Nazi) is not at all what one would use for the antecedent scenario for Y (he is not involved in Nazi intelligence operations on the Eastern Front). For, in selecting the most plausible scenario for the latter, one would likely select a scenario where he is still a Nazi, but simply has a different job. But, in selecting the most plausible scenario for the former, one would select a scenario where he is not a Nazi at all. This would require a longer scenario (and possibly a less unified one). As such, his non-involvement in NATO activities is only known to apply to the scenario where he is not a Nazi at all, but not known to apply to the scenario where he is a Nazi, but just had a different job in WWII. To put things differently, the consequent scenarios (Y and Z) are true based on, in part, the antecedent scenarios (X and Y). But, the antecedent scenarios (X and Y) are very different, and so the consequent scenario for one may not necessarily apply to the other. The truth of the premises does not guarantee the truth of the conclusion. As such, counterfactual transitivity is a pitfall of counterfactual reasoning.

The second fallacy is *counterfactual contraposition*. Consider a possible alliance structure between Syria and Iran, and how it might relate to Israel.

CF7. If Syria were to be more willing to work with Israel, then Iran would be more willing to work with Israel.

Therefore…

CF8. If Iran were not more willing to work with Israel, then Syria would not be more willing to work with Israel.

This is also a very attractive inference, since it is plainly a valid one in the case of a normal conditional statement.

NCF4. If Syria is an ally of Israel, then Syria is willing to work with Israel.

Therefore…

NCF5. If Syria is not willing to work with Israel, then Syria is not an ally of Israel.

In general, any conditional will imply its "contrapositive": a second conditional where the antecedent and consequent have switched positions and are negated. And, in the case of standard conditionals, if a conditional is true, its contrapositive will automatically also be true.

However, it is entirely possible for a counterfactual conditional to be true and for its contrapositive to be false. Suppose (for the sake of argument) that CF7 is true and that Syria's willingness to work with Israel also makes Iran more willing to work with Israel. That would not imply CF8. Perhaps Iran is only affected by Syria's actions, and not vice versa. Perhaps Syria would be willing to separate its relationship with Israel from Iran's. In that case, CF8 is false. Now, it is not the point of this example to show that it definitely would be false, but only that *the nature of counterfactuals does not guarantee that if CF7 were true then CF8 would also be true.* Thus, it is fallacious to reason from one to the other. To show that CF8 is true, one would have to argue for it directly (e.g., from noncounterfactuals).

More generally, the following form of reasoning is a counterfactual fallacy:

Fallacy of Counterfactual Contraposition;

1. If it were the case that X, then it would be the case that Y.

Does not automatically imply that:

2. If it were not the case that Y, then it would not be the case that X.

This does not mean that "2" is false, but only that "1" is not sufficient to show that "2" is true. Thus, if one were going to show that "2" is true, one would have to do so in a different way.

The third fallacy is *counterfactual antecedent strengthening*. Consider a nuclear-armed Syria and how it might relate to a nuclear-armed Saudi Arabia.

CF9. If Syria had nuclear weapons, then Syria would use them against Israel.

Therefore…

CF10. If Syria had nuclear weapons and Saudi Arabia had nuclear weapons, then Syria would use nuclear weapons against Israel.

This inference takes a conditional and then adds something to its antecedent. In general, this is valid with conditionals.

NCF6. If Syria has nuclear weapons, then Syria has WMDs.

Therefore…

NCF7. If Syria has nuclear weapons and Saudi Arabia has nuclear weapons, then Syria has WMDs.

The reason this is valid with normal conditionals is that (as in this example) the addition does nothing to affect the case one is considering. One still is considering the case where Syria has nuclear weapons, which is, in itself, enough to ensure they have WMDs. Whether or not another country has nuclear weapons simply makes no difference.

The reason this proves to be a fallacy is that the truth or falsity of a counterfactual depends very heavily on its antecedent scenario. And the antecedent scenario where Syria has nuclear weapons is not necessarily the same as the one where both Syria and Saudi Arabia have nuclear weapons. As such, it is entirely possible that, in the latter, all the major players have such weapons in the Middle East, and hence, all are unwilling to use them. Perhaps possessing these weapons has made all nations feel secure enough never to use them. Again, it is not the point of this example to assert that this is the case, but only to point out that if CF9 were true, that would not imply that CF10 were true; thus, this is a counterfactual fallacy.

More generally, the following form of reasoning is a counterfactual fallacy:

Fallacy of Counterfactual Antecedent Strengthening;

1. If it were the case that X, then it would be the case that Y.

   Do not automatically imply that,

2. If it were the case that X and it were the case that Z, then it would be the case that Y.

This does not mean that "2" is false, but only that "1" is not sufficient to show that "2" is true. Thus, if one were going to show that "2" is true, one would have to do so in a different way. These three fallacies are only a few examples of pitfalls in counterfactual reasoning. But, they are important to note. All three are very attractive, since they are valid in the case of normal conditionals. Counterfactual reasoners must discipline themselves to resist them.

More straw man arguments.

Appendix: The Process of Counterfactual Reasoning

Full and Abbreviated Lists of Counterfactual Reasoning Principles

Full list of all Twenty Principles

Counterfactual Reasoning Principle 1: *The degree to which one's ultimate counterfactual claim is justified is largely due to the extent to which one has structured the counterfactual reasoning process to address the most significant challenges to effective counterfactual reasoning.*

Counterfactual Reasoning Principle 2: *Any attempt to assess alternate possibilities, their consequences, and/or the relationships between them must begin by considering the antecedent scenario(s) that corresponds to the possibility in question.*

Counterfactual Reasoning Principle 3: *Possible antecedent scenarios should be generated with imagination and openness to many options, but with some preference for those that are shorter in temporal length, higher in triggering event probability, and higher in unity.*

Counterfactual Reasoning Principle 4: *Possible antecedent scenarios should be eliminated if they require either a violation of a well-established law of nature or an event that is extremely highly improbable (given all events immediately prior to it).*

Counterfactual Reasoning Principle 5: *Possible antecedent scenarios should be ranked (relative to each other) in terms of their temporal length, triggering event probability, and unity.*

Counterfactual Reasoning Principle 6: *If antecedent scenario S1 is superior to antecedent scenario S2 in more elements of plausibility that S2 is superior than S1, then S1 is more plausible than S2 (and is more reasonable to select than S2).*

Counterfactual Reasoning Principle 7: *If antecedent scenario S1 is superior to antecedent scenario S2 in one element of plausibility, and S2 is superior to S1 in terms of one element of plausibility, and S1 and S2 are tied in terms of one element of plausibility, but S1 has a greater degree of superiority to S2 (in the relevant element) than S2 has to S1 (in the relevant element), then S1 is more plausible than S2 (and is more reasonable to select than S2).*

Counterfactual Reasoning Principle 8: *After selecting an antecedent scenario, verify that the scenario captures the intention that was behind the consideration of the possibility in the first place.*

Counterfactual Reasoning Principle 9: *Possible intermediate states should be generated by identifying the sequence(s) of events that occurred (or are projected to occur) between the antecedent scenario and the consequent scenario as well as the probability of each of those events.*

Counterfactual Reasoning Principle 10: *Possible intermediate states should be assessed in order of the time at which they occurred (or are projected to occur) and by means of comparing their original probability to their probability given the antecedent scenario and any prior intermediate states.*

Counterfactual Reasoning Principle 11: *If a possible intermediate state's probability given the antecedent scenario (and any prior intermediate states) is exactly the same as its original probability, then it is reasonable to include as an intermediate state.*

Counterfactual Reasoning Principle 12: *If a possible intermediate state's probability given the antecedent scenario (and any prior intermediate states) is exactly greater than its original probability, then it is reasonable to include as an intermediate state.*

Counterfactual Reasoning Principle 13: *If a possible intermediate state's probability given the antecedent scenario (and any prior intermediate states) is not exactly greater and not exactly the same as its original probability, but still sufficiently high, then it is reasonable to include as an intermediate state.*

Counterfactual Reasoning Principle 14: *If a possible intermediate state could qualify as part of a consequent scenario of a counterfactual with the same antecedent (and antecedent scenario) as the one under consideration (it is part of a reasonable "supporting counterfactual"), then it is reasonable to include as an intermediate state.*

Counterfactual Reasoning Principle 15: *In assessing possible events that would be part of a supporting counterfactual, one should consider events that did not occur (or were not projected to occur) without the antecedent scenario.*

Counterfactual Reasoning Principle 16: *Counterfactual Reasoning Principle 16: Possible consequent scenarios should be generated by identifying all the sequences of events that are consistent with (i.e., do not contradict) the events of the intermediate states, antecedent scenarios, and history prior to that.*

Counterfactual Reasoning Principle 17: *Possible consequent scenarios should be assessed by identifying how frequently (or in what proportion) a particular event occurs in all the sequences of events that are consistent with (i.e., do not contradict) the events of the intermediate states, antecedent scenarios, and history prior to that.*

Counterfactual Reasoning Principle 18: *Possible consequent scenarios should be selected by first looking for events (of interest) that do not occur in any of the sequences of events that are consistent with (i.e., do not contradict) the events of the intermediate states, antecedent scenarios, and history prior to that. The nonoccurrence of any such events will be part of all consequent scenarios.*

Counterfactual Reasoning Principle 19: *If an event has a nontrivial nonzero probability of occurring, given the events of the intermediate states, antecedent scenarios, and history prior to that, then that event is reasonable to accept as part of a consequent scenario that might occur (and hence be considered as a consequence in decision making under uncertainty). This is true even if that event's probability is otherwise not ascertainable.*

Counterfactual Reasoning Principle 20: *If an event has a nonzero and ascertainable probability of occurring given the events of the intermediate states, antecedent scenarios, and history prior to that, then that event is reasonable to accept as part of a consequent scenario that would occur (and hence be considered as a consequence in decision making under risk).*

Abbreviated List of Counterfactual Reasoning Principles (In More Summary Fashion)

1. Generate possible ways the antecedent might come (or have come) to be. Remain open to many imaginative possibilities, but do not postulate anything that a) violates a known law of nature, or b) is extremely highly improbable.

2. Rank these possible ways in terms of how long they are, how probable their first event is, and how many distinct series of events converge to generate the antecedent (i.e., the three elements of plausibility).

3. Select the possible way that is superior to others in terms of more of the three elements of plausibility.

4. Generate possible events that occur after antecedent but before the time of interest to the analyst by identifying those that actually occurred (or are projected to occur) during that time period.

5. Select events whose probability given the antecedent (and any prior selected events) is greater than, unaffected by, of still sufficiently high relative to, its probability without the antecedent (and any prior selected events).

6. Select any event that is the consequent of a (would) counterfactual with the same antecedent as the one under consideration (and specify the probability).

7. Generate possible outcomes of the counterfactual (events that occur at the time of interest to the analyst) by identifying all events that are consistent with those postulated by steps 1-6.

8. Separate events that into those that have an ascertainable probability from those that do not have an ascertainable probability of occurring.

9. Select as a consequent of a "would" counterfactual any event that has an ascertainable probability of occurring (and specify the probability). This grounds a counterfactual for decision making under risk.

10. Select as a consequent of a "might" counterfactual any event that has a nonzero and nontrivial (even if otherwise not ascertainable) probability of occurring. This grounds a counterfactual for decision making under uncertainty.

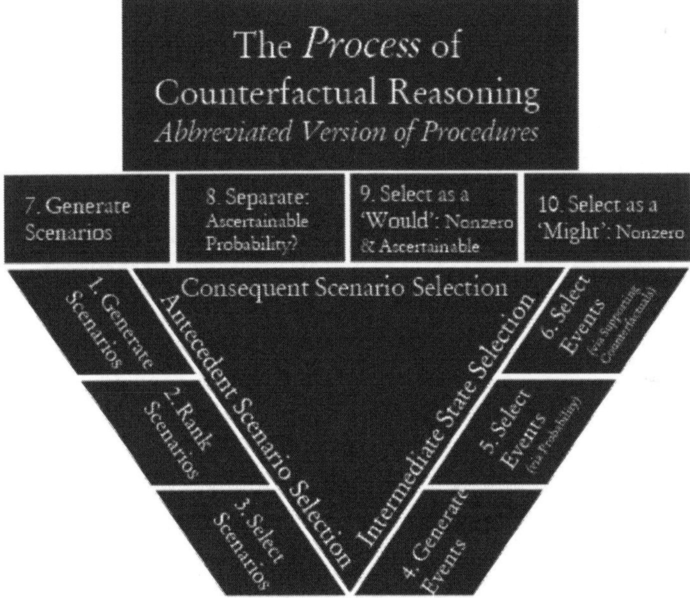

Figure 5: Chart representing the process of counterfactual reasoning (on the abbreviated summary version of the twenty principles). Note the shape. It has several meanings. From one perspective, the chart appears to be an arrow going down pointing one's attention to antecedent scenario selection and intermediate state selection. Since these two are the most critical (albeit counterintuitive) aspects of counterfactual reasoning, they deserve to be the object of attention. From another perspective, the chart appears to be a sort of bridge moving from steps 7 to 10 with steps 1 to 6 being supports for it. Since steps 1 to 6 lie underneath the surface, and are essential to moving from 7 to 10, this is also an appropriate way to conceive of this chart.

Glossary

Key Counterfactual Reasoning Terms

Antecedent: The first part of a counterfactual that forms the alternate possibility being considered. It is the "X" in "If X were to occur, then Y would (or might) occur."

Antecedent Scenario: The way in which the antecedent comes to be. It is the "back-story" of the counterfactual. In the case of a future possibility, this scenario would be a complete story from the present (or even further back) that leads up to the moment at which the antecedent becomes true. In the case of a past alternate possibility, this scenario would begin with a deviation from actual history and then chart an alternate course of history up until the time at which the antecedent becomes true.

Antecedent Scenario Selection (a.k.a. Selection of Antecedent Scenarios): The process of determining which of many possible antecedent scenarios is the most reasonable one to affirm.

Consequent: The second part of a counterfactual that forms the purported consequences of the alternate possibility being considered. It is the "Y" in "If X were to occur, then Y would (or might) occur."

Consequent Scenario: The way in which the consequent is true and the events that (immediately) follow its becoming true.

Consequent Scenario Selection (a.k.a. Selection of Consequent Scenarios): The process of determining which consequents stand in the "would" or "might" relationship with the antecedent.

Counterfactual: A conditional claim about an alternate possibility and its consequences of the form "If X were to occur, then Y would (or might) occur." Counterfactuals can refer to any subjunctive conditional (i.e., they include both past and future alternate possibilities).

Counterfactual Dependence: When one event would not have occurred if a prior event had not occurred. Y is counterfactually dependent on X. If X had not occurred, then Y would not have occurred. Many hold that counterfactual dependence between two events implies a causal relation between those events.

Determinism: Thesis that every event is the inevitable effect of prior causal factors. In other words, every event has a cause that increases its probability to 1. No event occurs uncaused or had any probability of not occurring.

Deterministic Biases: Human tendency to assume events occur in a deterministic world, when they do not. Examples are *foresight bias* and *hindsight bias.*

Elements of Plausibility: The three factors that are compared in order to select antecedent scenarios: *temporal length*, *triggering event probability*, and *unity.*

Foresight Bias: Human tendency to regard future events as inevitable when they are not (or more probable than they are).

Hindsight Bias: Human tendency to regard past events as having been inevitable when they were not (or more probable than they were).

Indeterminism: Thesis that not every event is the inevitable effect of prior causal factors. In other words, some events lack a cause that increases their probability to 1. Some events occur uncaused or had some probability of not occurring. The latter of these two fuel many counterfactuals.

Intermediate State: The events that make up the period of time after the antecedent becomes true but before the consequent becomes true. They are either 1) events that actually happened after the time at which the antecedent would be true (in the case of a past alternate possibility, 2) these events could be independently projected to happen after the time at which the antecedent would become true (in the case of a future alternate possibility), or 3) events that are the consequents of other true counterfactuals that have the same antecedents as the one under consideration.

Intermediate State Selection (a.k.a. Selection of Intermediate States): The process of determining what intermediate states to include in assessing a counterfactual.

Might: One of two ways that a consequence can be related to a particular alternate possibility. In the view of this work, to say that something "might" happen means that the event has a nonzero and nontrivial probability of occurring given the antecedent scenario and intermediate states (and thus is worthy of consideration as a possible consequence by means of decision making under uncertainty).

Modal Connection: The way in which the antecedent and consequent in a counterfactual are related (how the alternate possibility and their consequences are related). It is the "would" or "might" in "If X were to occur, then Y would (or might) occur."

Original Probability: Probability of an event without any postulation of the antecedent, antecedent scenario, or any resulting changes. It is the probability of event apart from the counterfactual situation.

Supporting Counterfactual: A counterfactual that has the same antecedent as the one under consideration but has a consequent that occurs earlier than the consequent in the one under consideration. Supporting counterfactuals can provide intermediate states for the counterfactuals they support.

Temporal Length: The period of time from the first alteration of actual history (or the present) to the time that the antecedent becomes true. One of the three elements used to determine the plausibility of an antecedent scenario.

Triggering Event: Event postulated in an antecedent scenario that is not attributed (causally) to any prior events different from actual history (or the present). It is an imagined change that is not due to any prior imagined change.

Triggering Event Probability: The probability of a *triggering event*. One of the three elements used to determine the plausibility of an antecedent scenario.

Unity: The number of different sequences of events that converge to bring about the antecedent in the antecedent scenario. The number of sequences is based upon the number of triggering events. One of the three elements used to determine the plausibility of an antecedent scenario.

Would: One of two ways that a consequence can be related to a particular alternate possibility. In the view of this work, to say that something "would" happen means that the event has a nonzero, nontrivial, and ascertainable probability of occurring given the antecedent scenario and intermediate states (and thus is worthy of consideration as a possible consequence by means of decision making under risk). To say that something "would" happen should always include some modifier estimating the probability of its occurring.

Endnotes

1. Some hold that "were/would" conditionals (those about past possibilities) should be categorized differently from "does/will" conditionals (those about future possibilities). Suffice it to say that this author agrees that there is a difference between the two *metaphysically*, but would (and will) contend that there is reason to treat them the same *epistemologically*.
2. For a different argument about the centrality of counterfactual reasoning, as well as a more general model of reasoning methods in intelligence, see Hendrickson 2008b.
3. For a brief overview of some of these methods and their (typically) perceived place in intelligence analysis, see Davis 2008; George 2006.
4. For example, Bennett 2003; Collins, Hall, and Paul 2004; Fearon 1991; Ferguson 1999; Kahneman 1995; Lewis 1973, 1979, 1986; Tetlock and Parker 2006b.
5. Supporting causal analysis might seem like it should be the most central role for counterfactual reasoning in intelligence analysis. However, there are some controversies about whether counterfactual dependence really does imply causal dependence. By contrast, there is no doubt (as shall be seen) about the other proposed roles for counterfactual reasoning. In addition, these other roles have no other means to support them (where as causal analysis does have other approaches that can be used for it besides counterfactual reasoning).
6. For example, Roese and Olson 1995a; Tetlock and Belkin 1996; Tetlock and Parker 2006a.
7. Consider the claims of the 9/11 Commission Report to this effect.
8. See Bennett 2003; Kvart 1986, 1992, 1996; Lewis 1973, 1979, 1986; Stalnaker 1968.
9. See Lewis 1973; Stalnaker 1968.
10. See Kahneman and Miller 1986; Kahneman 1995; McMullen, Markman, and Gavanski 1995; Roese and Olson 1995a, 1995b.

11. See Fearon 1991, 1996; Ferguson 1999; Lebow 2000, 2001; Tetlock and Belkin 1996; Tetlock 2006a, 2006b.

12. See Davis 2008; George 2006.

13. See Hendrickson 2008a.

14. Philosophers, or other purely academically motivated readers, should take note of both of these statements. The principles described here have been selected specifically because they make a difference to real-life reasoning (and not only to imaginative counterexamples). In addition, they are presented with only a very general line of reasoning in support of them, since the present concern is how to reason counterfactually rather than the justification of theories of counterfactual reasoning.

15. The principles described here replace any others that have previously advocated by this author, such as those in Hendrickson et al., 2008.

16. See Bennett 2003; Lewis 1973, 1979, 1986; Stalnaker 1968.

17. See Kvart 1986, 1992, 1994.

18. See Fearon 1991, 1996; Ferguson 1999; Lebow 2000, 2001; Tetlock and Belkin 1996; Tetlock 2006a, 2006b.

19. One might worry that this is biased in favor of more probable options. And, to a certain extent, it is. However, when one has to choose a possibility to consider, it makes sense to choose a more probable one, unless there is reason not to do so. Thus, if one selects an antecedent that is intrinsically more improbable, then so will be the antecedent scenarios. But, if there is room for scenarios that are less improbable, that is what will be selected.

20. One of the best discussions of this point occurs in Kvart 1986.

21. See Bennett 2003; Lewis 1973, 1979, 1986; Stalnaker 1968.

22. See Kvart 1986, 1992, 1994.

23. For example, Bennett 2003; Kvart 1986, 1992, 1996; Lewis 1973, 1979, 1986; Stalnaker 1968.

24. For more on basic decision making under risk, consider Hendrickson et. al. 2008.

25. For more on basic decision making under uncertainty, consider Hendrickson et. al. 2008.

26. Philosophers and other academics take note of this. The proposed account is driven by the need to ground strategic assessment, not merely to offer a theory of counterfactuals.

27. For more on basic generalization arguments, consider Hendrickson et al., 2008.

28. See Canton 2006; Cornish 2004; Georgantzas and Acar 1995; Naisbatt 1982; Ringland 1998; Schwartz 1991; Toffler 1970, 1980; van Der Heijden 2005.

29. See Lewis 1973; Kvart 1986. Although, it is important to note that there are major differences between these two approaches and the one that is advocated here, those may ultimately have implications for the logical systems they propose.

30. Note to the reader: this fallacy (as well as the other two to be discussed) also applies to "might" counterfactuals.

References

Bennett, Jonathan. 2003. *A Philosophical Guide to Conditionals.* Oxford University Press.

Canton, James. 2006. *The Extreme Future.* Dutton.

Collins, John, Ned Hall, and L.A. Paul. 2004. *Causation and Counterfactuals.* MIT Press.

Cornish, Edward. 2004. *Futuring: The Exploration of the Future.* World Futures Society.

Davis, Jack. 2008. "Why Bad Things Happen to Good Analysts." In Roger Z. George and James B. Bruce (eds.) *Analyzing Intelligence: Origins, Obstacles, and Innovations.* Georgetown University Press, 157-170.

Elster, Jon. 1978. *Logic and Society: Contradictions and Possible Worlds.* Wiley & Sons.

Fearon, James. 1991. "Counterfactuals and Hypothesis Testing in Political Science." *World Politics* 43: 169-95.

———. 1996. "Causes and Counterfactuals in Social Science." In Tetlock, Philip E. and Aaron Belkin (eds). *Counterfactual Thought Experiments in Global Politics: Logical, Methodological, and Psychological Perspectives.* Princeton University Press, 39-68.

Ferguson, Niall (ed). 1999. *Virtual History: Alternatives and Counterfactuals.* Basic Books.

Georgantzas, Nicholas C. and William Acar. 1995. *Scenario-Driven Planning.* Quorum Books.

George, Roger Z. 2006. "Fixing the Problem of Analytical Mindsets: Alternative Analysis." In George, Roger Z. and Robert D. Kline, (eds.) *Intelligence and the National Security Strategist.* Rowman and Littlefield, 327-340.

Goodman, Nelson. 1983. *Fact, Fiction, and Forecast.* Harvard University Press.

Hawthorn, Geoffrey. 1991. *Plausible Worlds: Possibility and Understanding in History and the Social Sciences.* Cambridge University Press.

Hendrickson, Noel. 2008a. "Counterfactual Reasoning, Structured Scenario Fusion, and Futures Analysis." In Auger, John D. and William L. Wimbish III, (eds.), *Proteus Futures Digest: Second Edition*, Proteus USA.

———. 2008b. "Critical Thinking in Intelligence Analysis." *International Journal for Intelligence and Counterintelligence.* Vol. 21, No. 4, 279-293.

———. forthcoming. "Applied Counterfactual Reasoning." In Howard Smith, Newton and Ammar Quasatiby (eds)., *Mathematical Models in Counterterrorism.* Springer.

Hendrickson, Noel and Kirk St. Amant, William Hawk,William O'Meara, and Daniel Flage. 2008. *Rowman and Littlefield's Handbook of Critical Thinking.* Rowman and Littlefield.

Kahneman, Daniel, and Dale Miller. 1986. "Norm Theory: Comparing Reality to Its Alternatives." *Psychological Review* 93: 136-153.

Kahneman, Daniel. 1995. "Varieties of Counterfactual Thinking." In Roese, Neal J. and James M. Olson (eds.) *The Social Psychology of Counterfactual Thinking.* Lawrence Erlbaum Associates, 375-396.

Kvart, Igal. 1986. *A Theory of Counterfactuals.* Hackett Publishing Company.

———. 1992. "Counterfactuals." *Erkenntnis* 36: 139-179.

———. 1994. "Counterfactuals: Ambiguities, True Premises, and Knowledge." *Synthese* 100: 133-164.

Lebow, Richard Ned. 2000. "What's So Different About a Counterfactual?" *World Politics* 52: 550-585.

———. 2001. "Contingency, Catalysts, and International Systems Change." *Political Science Quarterly* Vol. 115, No. 4: 591-616.

Lewis, David. 1973. *Counterfactuals.* Basil Blackwell.

———. 1979. "Counterfactual Dependence and Time's Arrow." *Nous* 13: 455-476.

———. 1986. "Postscripts to "Counterfactual Dependence and Time's Arrow." In *Philosophical Papers, Vol. 2.* Oxford University Press, 52-66.

McMullen, Matthew N., Keith D. Markman, and Igor Gavanski. 1995. "Living in Neither the Best Nor the Worst of All Possible Worlds." In Roese, Neal J. and James M. Olson (eds.) *The Social Psychology of Counterfactual Thinking.* Lawrence Erlbaum Associates, 133-168.

Naisbatt, John. 1982. *Megatrends: Ten New Directions Transforming Our Lives.* Warner.

Ringland, Gill. 1998. *Scenario Planning.* Wiley & Sons.

Roese, Neal J. and James M. Olson. 1995a. "Counterfactual Thinking: A Critical Overview." In Roese, Neal J. and James M. Olson (eds.) *The Social Psychology of Counterfactual Thinking.* Lawrence Erlbaum Associates, 1-56.

———. 1995b. "Functions of Counterfactual Thinking." In Roese, Neal J. and James M. Olson (eds.) *The Social Psychology of Counterfactual Thinking.* Lawrence Erlbaum Associates, 169-198.

Schwartz, Peter. 1991. *The Art of the Long View: Planning for the Future in an Uncertain World.* Doubleday.

Stalnaker, Robert. 1968. "A Theory of Conditionals." In Nicholas Rescher (ed) *Studies in Logical Theory.* Oxford University Press.

Strasser, Steven (ed.) 2004. *The 9/11 Investigations.* Public Affairs Reports.

Tetlock, Philip E. and Aaron Belkin. 1996. "Counterfactual Thought Experiments in Global Politics: Logical, Methodological, and Psychological Perspectives." In Tetlock, Philip E. and Aaron Belkin (eds).

Counterfactual Thought Experiments in Global Politics: Logical, Methodological, and Psychological Perspectives. Princeton University Press, 3-38.

Tetlock, Philip E., and Geoffrey Parker. 2006a. "Counterfactual History." In Tetlock, Philip E., Richard Ned Lebow, and Geoffrey Parker (eds).

Unmaking the West: "What If" Scenarios That Rewrite World History. University of Michigan Press, 363-392.

____________. 2006b. "Counterfactual Thought Experiments." In Tetlock, Philip E.,

Richard Ned Lebow, and Geoffrey Parker (eds). *Unmaking the West: "What If" Scenarios That Rewrite World History.* University of MichiganPress, 14-46.

Toffler, Alvin. 1970. *Future Shock.* Random House.

____________. 1980. *The Third Wave.* William Morrow.

Van Der Heijden. 2005. *Scenarios: The Art of Strategic Conversation.* Wiley & Sons.

Weber, Max. 1949. *The Methodology of the Social Sciences.* FreePress of Glencoe.

Printed in Great Britain
by Amazon